Knit your own
Dolls

Over **35** patterns
for dolls & their outfits,
accessories, & pets

Fiona Goble

CICO BOOKS
LONDON NEW YORK

Published in 2018 by CICO Books
An imprint of Ryland Peters & Small Ltd
20–21 Jockey's Fields   341 E 116th St
London WC1R 4BW   New York, NY 10029

www.rylandpeters.com

10 9 8 7 6 5 4 3 2 1

A CIP catalog record for this book is available from the Library
of Congress and the British Library.

ISBN: 978-1-78249-563-5

Printed in China

Editor: Kate Haxell
Designer: Luana Gobbo
Photographer: Geoff Dann
Stylist: Nel Haynes

Art director: Sally Powell
Production controller: David Hearn
Publishing manager: Penny Craig
Publisher: Cindy Richards

contents

introduction

The best thing about knitting the dolls from this book is that you can make them look just how you want. I've knitted an array of characters, each with a unique style. There's a hipster, a land girl, a little boy ready for bed—and even a magical little girl with a unicorn horn. And I'm really pleased with how they turned out.

But perhaps you're after something different.

So if you want a doll with long mauve hair, a girlie dress, a cool blazer, long boots, a beanie hat, and a pet rabbit—no problem! Browse through the patterns, make your list, sort out your colors, and you're ready to go.

Or perhaps you want to knit a doll that looks like your friend, grandson, daughter, or co-worker. Again, take a look through the pages, choose your colors and pick out the sort of clothes they wear. It's not just simple, it's also great fun.

The second best thing about knitting dolls—and I nearly made this the very best thing—is the way their personalities develop as you sew them together, embroider their features, give them a hair style, and create their outfits. Perhaps it's just me and the fact that I never quite got over that phase of making dolls' clothes. It hit me first when I was about six years old and never really left.

But I don't think that's it. These days, almost everyone seems keen to try their hand at crafting, and with stores crammed full of mass-produced items, a handmade gift seems so much more special.

This book's basic doll pattern is suitable for advanced-beginner knitters and beyond. Many of the outfits are also well within the abilities of advanced beginners. But there are a few that are more complicated—most noticeably those with fancy stitches or involving more than one color. So before you begin, have a read through the patterns that catch your eye and check that you feel comfortable with them.

Please also take a look at the Techniques section starting on page 114, where I have some useful advice on knitting the dolls, sewing them together, and adding the finishing touches.

If you have any comments or queries, please feel free to contact me via my website, fionagoble.com, where I will always do my best to help out. I've loved creating the dolls in this book and I hope you love creating your own versions just as much.

Basic Doll

This is the basic body for the dolls in this book. Each individual doll pattern will give the yarns needed to make that doll's body, plus any special instructions needed.

SIZE

Height of doll from heel to crown 11in (28cm)

ABBREVIATIONS

m1 below = Find the top loop of the stitch below the next stitch on the left-hand needle. Insert the tip of the right-hand needle into that top loop from front to back. If this is difficult try picking up the stitch from the back, hold it with the left thumb and forefinger, then remove the needle and reinsert it into the loop from front to back. Knit into the stitch then knit into the stitch on the needle (see page 121).

See also page 127

BODY AND HEAD

(MAKE 2)
Cast on 18 sts.
Work 28 rows in st st beg with a k row.
Row 29: [Ssk] 4 times, k2, [k2tog] 4 times. *(10 sts)*
Row 30: P2tog, p to last 2 sts, p2tog tbl. *(8 sts)*
Work 2 rows in st st beg with a k row.
Row 33: K1, [m1 below] twice, k2, [m1 below] twice, k1. *(12 sts)*
Row 34: Purl.
Row 35: K1, [m1 below] twice, k6, [m1 below] twice, k1. *(16 sts)*
Row 36: Purl.
Row 37: K1, [m1 below], k12, [m1 below], k1. *(18 sts)*
Work 13 rows in st st beg with a p row.
Row 51: K1, ssk, k to last 3 sts, k2tog, k1. *(16 sts)*
Row 52: Purl.
Rep rows 51–52 once more. *(14 sts)*
Row 55: K2, ssk, k6, k2tog, k2. *(12 sts)*
Bind (cast) off pwise.

ARMS

(MAKE 2)
Cast on 10 sts.
Work 28 rows in st st beg with a k row.
Row 29: K5, m1, turn, p1, turn, k1, turn, p1, turn, k to end. *(11 sts)*
Work 3 rows in st st beg with a p row.
Row 33: K1, ssk, k5, k2tog, k1. *(9 sts)*
Break yarn and thread it through rem sts.

LEGS

(MAKE 2)
Cast on 24 sts.
Work 4 rows in st st beg with a k row.
Row 5: K6, [ssk] 3 times, [k2tog] 3 times, k to end. *(18 sts)*
Row 6: Purl.
Row 7: K5, [ssk] twice, [k2tog] twice, k to end. *(14 sts)*
Row 8: Purl.
Row 9: K5, ssk, k2tog, k to end. *(12 sts)*
Work 29 rows in st st beg with a p row.
Bind (cast) off.

TO MAKE UP DOLL

Join side and top seams of body and head pieces using mattress stitch (page 126). Stuff, shaping the doll as you go. Close lower seam using mattress stitch.
Join sole of foot seam and back of leg seams using mattress stitch, leaving top ends open. Stuff and oversew (page 125) legs to outside edges of lower body.
Join hand and arm seams using mattress stitch, leaving top ends open. Stuff then oversew to sides of body about ½in (1.25cm) down from the thinnest part of the neck, with the arm seam facing the body with the thumb on the outside.

French Louise

Louise is in love with classic French fashion such as this Breton striped top and red Capri pants. With her feet nestled inside her classic ballet flats, she's all ready for a stroll to the local café with pet poodle, Chloé. So it'll be coffee and a croissant for Louise, and a bowl of water and perhaps a few crumbs for Chloé.

you will need

YARN AND MATERIALS

FOR DOLL

Debbie Bliss Baby Cashmerino (55% wool, 33% acrylic, 12% cashmere), 137yd (125m) per 1¾oz (50g) ball of sport weight (light DK) yarn
- ¾ ball of Clotted Cream 65 (A)— head and body, arms
- ¼ ball of Tobacco 98 (B)—hair
- ¼ ball of Royal 70 (C)—striped top
- ¼ ball of White 100 (D)—striped top
- ¼ ball of Red 34 (E)—Capri pants
- Small amount of Drake 302 (F)—shoes

Very small amount of coral, red, or pink embroidery floss (thread) or yarn—mouth

Very small amount of black yarn—eyes

Small readymade red ribbon bow

1oz (30g) polyester toy filling

FOR POODLE

Debbie Bliss Baby Cashmerino (55% wool, 33% acrylic, 12% cashmere), 137yd (125m) per 1¾oz (50g) ball of sport weight (light DK) yarn
- ¼ ball of Ecru 101 (G)—dog
- Small amount of Sea Green 99 (H)—dog leash

Plymouth Yarn Dreamland Fancy (97% acrylic, 3% nylon) 84yd (78m) per 1¾oz (50g) ball of bulky (chunky) weight bouclé yarn
- Small amount of Cream 6101 (J)—dog's fur

Small amount of polyester toy filling

NEEDLES AND EQUIPMENT

US3 (3.25mm) knitting needles (for all pieces other than poodle trim)

US6 (4mm) knitting needles (for poodle trim only)

D3 (3.25mm) crochet hook (or one of similar size)

Yarn sewing needle

Large-eyed embroidery needle

4 stitch markers or small safety pins

Pins

Coloring pencil in deep pink or red

GAUGE (TENSION)

Approximately 25 stitches and 34 rows to 4in (10cm) over st st (see also page 114)

ABBREVIATIONS

See page 127

main doll

Work as for basic pattern on page 9. Work head and body pieces, arms and legs in A.

HAIR

(MAKE 1)

Cast on 18 sts in B.

Work 8 rows in st st beg with a k row.

Row 9: Ssk, k to last 2 sts, k2tog. *(16 sts)*

Row 10: Purl.

Rep rows 9–10 twice more. *(12 sts)*

Row 15: Inc, k to last 2 sts, inc, k1. *(14 sts)*

Row 16: Purl.

Rep rows 15–16 once more. *(16 sts)*

Rep row 15 once more. *(18 sts)*

Row 20: P5, bind (cast) off 8 sts pwise, p to end. *(2 groups of 5 sts)*

Work on 5 sts just worked only, leaving rem sts on needle.

Next row: K3, k2tog. *(4 sts)*

Work 3 rows in st st beg with a p row.

Next row: K3, m1, k1. *(5 sts)*

Next row: Purl.

Next row: K4, m1, k1. *(6 sts)*

Next row: Purl.

Bind (cast) off.

Rejoin yarn to rem 5 sts on RS of work.

Next row: Ssk, k to end. *(4 sts)*

Work 3 rows in st st beg with a p row.

Next row: K1, m1, k to end. *(5 sts)*

Next row: Purl.

Rep last 2 rows once more. *(6 sts)*

Bind (cast) off.

TO MAKE UP DOLL

Make up main doll as explained on page 9. For eyes, work French knots (see page 124) using black yarn. Embroider mouth in straight stitch (see page 124) using embroidery floss (thread) or a separated strand of yarn. Work nose by working a couple of chain stitches (see page 124) in A, in a short vertical line. To make the nose slightly more prominent, work another couple of chain stitches over the ones you have just sewn. Add a bit of color to the cheeks using the coloring pencil. Seam the hair piece to form a cap shape. Pin then oversew (see page 125) the hair piece to head, using matching yarn. Weave in all loose ends. Stitch bow in place using the photograph as a guide.

striped top

FRONT AND BACK

The top is knitted from the shoulder down.
(MAKE 2)
Cast on 18 sts in C.
Row 1: Knit.
Work 2 rows in st st beg with a k row.
Leave C at side and join in D.
Work 2 rows in st st beg with a k row.
Rep last 4 rows once more.
Row 10: In C, k2, m1, k to last 2 sts, m1, k2. *(20 sts)*
Row 11: Purl.
In D, work 2 rows in st st beg with a k row.
Mark beg and end of last row with stitch markers or small safety pins.
Rep rows 10–13 (last 4 rows) once more. *(22 sts)*
Work 6 more rows in st st keeping to the striped patt.
Knit 2 rows in C.
Bind (cast) off.

SLEEVES

(MAKE 2)
Cast on 18 sts in C.
Row 1: Knit.
Work 2 rows in st st beg with a k row.
Leave C at side and join in D.
Work 20 rows in st st, keeping to the striped patt as for Front and Back.
Bind (cast) off.

TO MAKE UP TOP

Sew side seams from lower edge to stitch markers. Sew ⅜in (1cm) along each side of top edge to form shoulder seams. Sew sleeve seams. Insert sleeves into armholes and sew in place from the inside. Weave in all loose ends.

capri pants

(MAKE 1)
Cast on 18 sts in E.
Row 1: Knit.
Work 22 rows in st st beg with a k row.
Break yarn and leave sts on needle.
Cast on 18 sts on empty needle.
Row 1: Knit.
Work 22 rows in st st beg with a k row but do not break yarn.
Now work across all 36 sts.
Work 14 rows in st st beg with a k row.
Next row: [K1, p1] to end.
Rep last row once more.
Bind (cast) off keeping to the k1, p1 patt.

TO MAKE UP PANTS

Sew inside leg and back seams. Weave in all loose ends.

shoes

(MAKE 2)
Cast on 24 sts in F.
Work 4 rows in st st beg with a k row.
Row 5: K6, [ssk] 3 times, [k2tog] 3 times, k to end. *(18 sts)*
Bind (cast) off pwise.

TO MAKE UP SHOES

Fold shoe piece in half so that the right side is on the inside and oversew (see page 125) sole. Turn the piece the right way out and sew the back seam. Weave in all loose ends.

chloé the poodle

BODY AND HEAD

(MAKE 1)
Cast on 10 sts in G.
Row 1: Inc, k to last 2 sts, inc, k1. *(12 sts)*
Row 2: Purl.
Rep rows 1–2, 3 times more. *(18 sts)*
Work 4 rows in st st beg with a k row.
Row 13: K9, turn and cast on 10 sts for back of neck, turn back and k to end. *(28 sts)*
Row 14: Purl.
Row 15: K1, ssk, k to last 3 sts, k2tog, k1. *(26 sts)*
Row 16: Purl.
Row 17: K1, [ssk] twice, k to last 5 sts, [k2tog] twice, k1. *(22 sts)*
Row 18: Purl.
Row 19: Bind (cast) off 4 sts, k to end. *(18 sts)*
Row 20: Bind (cast) off 4 sts pwise, p to end. *(14 sts)*

Row 21: Bind (cast) off 2 sts, k to end. *(12 sts)*
Row 22: Bind (cast) off 2 sts pwise, p to end. *(10 sts)*
Row 23: K1, ssk, k4, k2tog, k1. *(8 sts)*
Row 24: P2tog, p4, p2tog tbl. *(6 sts)*
Row 25: K1, ssk, k2tog, k1. *(4 sts)*
Break yarn, thread through rem sts, and secure.

FRONT LEGS
(MAKE 2)
Cast on 6 sts in G.
Work 10 rows in st st beg with a k row.
Row 11: [K2tog] 3 times. *(3 sts)*
Break yarn, thread through rem sts, and secure.

BACK LEGS
(MAKE 2)
Cast on 6 sts in G.
Work 6 rows in st st beg with a k row.
Row 7: K1, m1, k to last st, m1, k1. *(8 sts)*
Row 8: Purl.
Rep rows 7–8 twice more. *(12 sts)*
Work 2 rows in st st beg with a k row.
Row 15: K1, ssk, k to last 3 sts, k2tog, k1. *(10 sts)*
Row 16: P2tog, p to last 2 sts, p2tog tbl. *(8 sts)*
Bind (cast) off.

FUR TRIM FOR BODY
(MAKE 1)
Using US6 (4mm) needles, cast on 14 sts in J.
Knit 2 rows.
Row 3: Bind (cast) off 2 sts, k to end. *(12 sts)*
Rep row 3 once more. *(10 sts)*
Row 5: Cast on 1 st, k to end. *(11 sts)*
Rep row 5 once more. *(12 sts)*
Row 7: Bind (cast) off 4 sts, k to end. *(8 sts)*
Rep row 7 once more. *(4 sts)*
Knit 4 rows.
Row 13: [K2tog] twice. *(2 sts)*
Row 14: K2tog. *(1 st)*
Fasten off.

FUR TRIM FOR LEGS
(MAKE 4)
Using US6 (4mm) needles, cast on 5 sts in J.
Bind (cast) off.

EARS
(MAKE 2)
Using US6 (4mm) needles, cast on 3 sts in J.
Knit 5 rows.
Bind (cast) off.

TOP KNOT
(MAKE 1)
Using US6 (4mm) needles, cast on 4 sts in J.
Knit 4 rows.
Bind (cast) off.

MAIN TAIL
(MAKE 1)
Using D3 (3.25mm) crochet hook and G, work a ⅜in (1cm) crochet chain (see page 125).

TAIL BOBBLE
Using US 6 (4mm) needles, cast on 2 sts in J.
Knit 2 rows.
Bind (cast) off.

TO MAKE UP POODLE
Fold head and body piece in half so that the right sides are facing outward. Sew seam that forms back of neck. Sew lower seam, leaving opening on lower side of body for stuffing. Stuff and close gap.
Fold back legs in half and seam, stuffing as you go. Do the same for the front legs. Stitch limbs in place. Oversew body fur trim in place around front of body and front legs, using the photograph as a guide. Sew fur trims for legs into small circles then stitch in place on the lower part of the legs. Sew ears in place. Work small running stitches around the outside of the topknot piece and gather into a small sphere, adding a bit of stuffing as you go. Stitch in place between the ears. Make bobble for tail in the same way as you made topknot then stitch in place on one end of the main tail. Stitch the tail in place.
For eyes, work two French knots (see page 124) using a separated strand of black yarn. Using a separated strand of black yarn, work a small circle of chain stitches (see page 124) for the nose. Add a vertical straight stitch (see page 124) beneath the nose. Weave in all loose ends.

DOG LEASH
Using D3 (3.25mm) crochet hook and H, make an 11-in (28-cm) crochet chain. Secure one end around the poodle's neck and make a loop at the other end for the handle.

Sportswear Sam

Sam loves keeping fit and he loves playing and watching all kinds of sports. But more than anything he loves shopping for the latest sports gear and accessories — and showing them off to his friends. Anyone for tennis or perhaps a gentle jog round the park?

main doll

Work as for basic pattern on page 9. Work head and body pieces, arms and legs in A.

HAIR
(MAKE 1)
Cast on 18 sts in B.
Work 4 rows in st st beg with a k row.
Row 5: Ssk, k to last 2 sts, k2tog. *(16 sts)*
Row 6: Purl.
Rep last 2 rows twice more. *(12 sts)*
Row 11: Inc, k to last 2 sts, inc, k1. *(14 sts)*
Row 12: P5, turn. *(5 sts)*
Work on 5 sts just worked only, leaving rem sts on needle.
Next row: K to last 2 sts, inc, k1. *(6 sts)*
Next row: Purl.
Next row: Ssk, k2, inc, k1.
Next row: P to last 2 sts, p2tog tbl. *(5 sts)*
Next row: Ssk, k to end. *(4 sts)*
Next row: P to last 2 sts, p2tog tbl. *(3 sts)*
Next row: Ssk, k1. *(2 sts)*
Next row: P2tog. *(1 st)*
Fasten off.
Rejoin yarn to rem 9 sts on WS of work.
Next row: Purl.
Next row: Inc, k to end. *(10 sts)*

Next row: Bind (cast) off 3 sts pwise, p to end. *(7 sts)*
Next row: Inc, k4, k2tog.
Next row: Bind (cast) off 2 sts pwise, p to end. *(5 sts)*
Next row: K3, k2tog. *(4 sts)*
Next row: P2tog, p2. *(3 sts)*
Next row: K1, k2tog. *(2 sts)*
Next row: P2tog. *(1 st)*
Fasten off.

TO MAKE UP DOLL
Make up main doll as explained on page 9. For eyes, work French knots (see page 124) using black yarn. Embroider mouth in straight stitch (see page 124) using embroidery floss (thread) or a separated strand of yarn. Work nose by working a couple of chain stitches (see page 124) in A, in a short vertical line. To make the nose slightly more prominent, work another couple of chain stitches over the ones you have just sewn. For the ears, work a few chain stitches in A, in a short vertical line at the side of the head, in line with the eyes. Then work another row of chain stitches on top to make the ears a bit more prominent. Add a bit of color to the cheeks using the coloring pencil.
Seam the hair piece to form a cap shape. Pin then oversew (see page 125) the hair piece to head, using matching yarn.
Weave in all loose ends.

you will need

YARN AND MATERIALS
Debbie Bliss Baby Cashmerino (55% wool, 33% acrylic, 12% cashmere), 137yd (125m) per 1¾oz (50g) ball of sport weight (light DK) yarn
  ¾ ball of Mink 64 (A)—head and body, arms, and legs
  ¼ ball of Chocolate 11 (B)—hair
  ½ ball of Drake 302 (C)—top
  ¼ ball of White 100 (D)—shorts and stripes on top
  ¼ ball of Red 34 (E)—baseball cap, stripes on shorts, bag trim
  Small amount of Acid Yellow 91 (F)—shoes
  Small amount of Mint 03 (G)—bag
  Very small amount of Black 300—eyes and shoe laces

Very small amount of coral, red, or pink embroidery floss (thread) or yarn—mouth

1oz (30g) polyester toy filling

NEEDLES AND EQUIPMENT
US3 (3.25mm) knitting needles
D3 (3.25mm) crochet hook (or one of similar size)
Yarn sewing needle
Large-eyed embroidery needle
Coloring pencil in deep pink or red
4 stitch markers or small safety pins

GAUGE (TENSION)
Approximately 25 stitches and 34 rows to 4in (10cm) over st st (see also page 114)

ABBREVIATIONS
See page 127

top

FRONT AND BACK

(MAKE 2)

Cast on 22 sts in C.

Row 1: Knit.

Leave C at side and join in D.

Work 2 rows in st st beg with a k row.

Break D and cont in C.

Work 14 rows in st st beg with a
k row.

Mark beg and end of last row with
small safety pins or stitch markers.

Row 18: K2, ssk, k to last 4 sts,
k2tog, k2. *(20 sts)*

Row 19: Purl.

Rep rows 18–19 once more. *(18 sts)*

Work 6 rows in st st beg with a k row.

Row 28: Bind (cast) off 3 sts, k to last
3 sts, bind (cast) off to end. *(12 sts)*

Cut and rejoin D to rem 12 sts on WS
of work.

Row 29: Purl.

Bind (cast) off loosely, pwise.

SLEEVES

Join neck edges and shoulders of
front and back pieces. With RS facing
and C, pick up and knit 9 sts from one
safety pin or marker to shoulder edges
and another 9 sts from shoulder edges
to second safety pin or marker. Work
7 rows in st st beg with a p row. Leave
C at side and join in D.

Work 2 rows in st st beg with a k row.

Break D and work rem of sleeve in C.

Knit 2 rows.

Bind (cast) off.

Rep for second sleeve.

TO MAKE UP TOP

Join side and sleeve seams. Using D,
embroider number in chain stitch (see
page 124). Weave in all loose ends.

shorts

(MAKE 1)

Cast on 18 sts in D.

Work 13 rows in st st beg with a
p row.

Break yarn.

Cast on 18 sts on empty needle.

Work 13 rows in st st beg with a p row
but do not break yarn.

Now work across all 36 sts.

Work 13 rows in st st beg with a
k row.

Next row: [K1, p1] to end.

Rep last row once more.

Bind (cast) off keeping to the k1, p1
patt.

TO MAKE UP SHORTS

Sew inside leg and back seams. Using
E, work a row of chain stitch (see page
124) up the outside of each leg of the
shorts, using the photograph as a
guide. Weave in all loose ends.

baseball cap

(MAKE 1)
Cast on 36 sts in E.
Work 10 rows in st st beg with a
k row.
Row 11: [K2tog] to end. *(18 sts)*
Row 12: Purl.
Row 13: [K2tog] to end. *(9 sts)*
Row 14: [P2tog] twice, p1, [p2tog]
twice. *(5 sts)*
Break yarn, thread through rem sts,
and secure.

TO MAKE UP AND WORK PEAK
Sew the back seam of cap before
working the peak.

PEAK
With RS facing, using E, pick up and
knit 16 sts across the center front of
the cap.
Row 1: P2 tog, p to last 2 sts, p2tog
tbl. *(14 sts)*
Row 2: K1, ssk, k to last 3 sts, k2tog,
k1. *(12 sts)*
Row 3: P2tog, p to last 2 sts, p2tog
tbl. *(10 sts)*
Rep rows 2–3 once more. *(6 sts)*
Row 6: K1, m1, k to last st, m1, k1.
(8 sts)
Row 7: P1, m1 pwise, p to last st, m1
pwise, p1. *(10 sts)*
Rep rows 6–7 once more. *(14 sts)*
Rep row 6 once more. *(16 sts)*
Row 11: Purl.
Bind (cast) off.
Fold the peak in half to the inside
of the cap and oversew the sides
and the bound- (cast-) off edge under
the brim.

shoes

(MAKE 2)
Cast on 26 sts in F.
Work 4 rows in st st beg with a k row.
Row 5: K7, [ssk] 3 times, [k2tog]
3 times, k to end. *(20 sts)*
Row 6: Purl.
Row 7: K6, [ssk] twice, [k2tog] twice,
k to end. *(16 sts)*
Row 8: Knit.
Bind (cast) off.

TO MAKE UP SHOES
Fold shoe pieces in half with right side
on inside and oversew (see page 125)
sole. Turn pieces the right way out and
sew back seams. Using black yarn,
work two straight stitches (see page
124) on front of shoes to represent
laces. Weave in all loose ends.

duffel bag

BASE
(MAKE 1)
Cast on 5 sts in G.
Row 1: Inc, k to last 2 sts, inc, k1.
(7 sts)
Row 2: Purl.
Rep rows 1–2, 3 times more. *(13 sts)*
Row 9: Knit.
Row 10: Purl.
Row 11: Ssk, k to last 2 sts, k2tog.
(11 sts)
Row 12: Purl.
Rep rows 11–12 twice more. *(7 sts)*
Row 17: Ssk, k to last 2 sts, k2tog.
(5 sts)
Bind (cast) off pwise.

SIDES
Cast on 32 sts in G.
Work 4 rows in st st beg with a k row.
Leave G at side and join in E.
Work 2 rows in st st beg with a k row.
Break E and work rem of item in G.
Work 13 rows in st st beg with a
k row.
Row 20: Knit.
Bind (cast) off.

DRAWSTRING
(MAKE 1)
Using crochet hook and E, work
an 8-in (20-cm) crochet chain (see
page 125).

TO MAKE UP BAG
Join main seam of side piece. Join
side piece to base from the inside.
Thread drawstring in and out around
top of main piece of bag, beginning by
seam. Pull ends level then secure to
bag by base of main seam.

Sophia Loves Science

Sophia loves nothing more than donning her white lab coat, sorting out her test tubes, pipettes, and petri dishes, and getting down to a bit of experimentation. But she loves clothes, too, and doesn't want to turn up to the lab in anything drab.

you will need

YARN AND MATERIALS

Debbie Bliss Baby Cashmerino (55% wool, 33% acrylic, 12% cashmere), 137yd (125m) per 1¾oz (50g) ball of sport weight (light DK) yarn

¾ ball Camel 102 (A)—head and body, arms, legs

¼ ball Black 300 (B)—hair, eyes

¼ ball Citrus 18 (C)—top

¼ ball Fuchsia 88 (D)—pants

½ ball Mist 57 (E)—pants

½ ball White 100 (F)—lab coat

Small amount of Acid Yellow 91 (G)—shoes

Small amount of Silver 12 (H)— safety goggles

Very small amount of coral, red, or pink embroidery floss (thread) or yarn—mouth

1 x ⅜in (10mm) green button

3 x ⁵⁄₁₆in (8mm) pale gray buttons

2 x small silver beads

Small amount of thick, clear acetate

PVA glue

Small amount of waxed paper

1oz (30g) polyester toy filling

NEEDLES AND EQUIPMENT

US3 (3.25mm) knitting needles

D3 (3.25mm) crochet hook (or one of similar size)

J10 (6mm) crochet hook (or one of similar size)

Yarn sewing needle

Large-eyed embroidery needle

Pins

Coloring pencil in deep pink or red

GAUGE (TENSION)

Approximately 25 stitches and 34 rows to 4in (10cm) over st st (see also page 114)

ABBREVIATIONS

See page 127

main doll

Work as for basic pattern on page 9. Work head and body pieces, arms and legs in A.

HAIR

(MAKE 1)

Cast on 19 sts in B.

Row 1: K1, [p1, k1] to end.

Rep row 1, 3 times more.

Row 5: P2tog, [k1, p1] to last 3 sts, k1, p2tog tbl. *(17 sts)*

Row 6: P1, [k1, p1] to end.

Row 7: Ssk, [p1, k1] to last 3 sts, p1, k2tog. *(15 sts)*

Row 8: K1, [p1, k1] to end.

Rep rows 5–6 once more. *(13 sts)*

Row 11: Inc pwise, [k1, p1] to last 2 sts, k1, inc pwise. *(15 sts)*

Row 12: K1, [p1, k1] to end.

Row 13: Inc, [p1, k1] to last 2 sts, p1, inc. *(17 sts)*

Row 14: P1, [k1, p1] to end.

Row 15: Inc pwise, [k1, p1] twice, bind (cast) off 7 sts, keeping to the k1, p1 patt, (1 st rem on needle from binding/casting off), k1, p1, k1, inc pwise. *(12 sts)*

Work on last group of 6 sts only, leaving rem sts on needle.

Next row: [K1, p1] twice, ssk. *(5 sts)*

Next row: P2tog, k1, p1, k1. *(4 sts)*

Next row: K1, p1, k2tog. *(3 sts)*

Next row: P2tog, k1. *(2 sts)*

Next row: K2tog. *(1 st)*

Fasten off.

Rejoin yarn to rem 6 sts on WS of work.

Next row: K2tog, [p1, k1] twice. *(5 sts)*
Next row: K1, p1, k1, p2tog. *(4 sts)*
Next row: K2tog, p1, k1. *(3 sts)*
Next row: K1, p2tog. *(2 sts)*
Next row: K2tog. *(1 st)*
Fasten off.

BRAID (PLAIT)
(MAKE 1)
Using the J10 (6mm) crochet hook and four 1¾-yd (1.6-m) lengths of B together, work a 10-in (25.5-cm) crochet chain (see page 125). Fasten off leaving long ends.

TO MAKE UP DOLL
Make up main doll as explained on page 9.
For eyes, work French knots (see page 124) using B. Embroider mouth in straight stitch (see page 124) using embroidery floss (thread) or a separated strand of yarn. Work nose by working a couple of chain stitches (see page 124) in A, in a short vertical line. To make the nose slightly more prominent, work another couple of chain stitches over the ones you have just sewn. Add a bit of color to the cheeks using the coloring pencil. Seam the hair piece to form a cap shape. Pin then oversew (see page 125) the hair piece to head, using matching yarn. Sew braid (plait) across top of head, using photograph as a guide and fray braid ends.
Weave in all loose ends.

top

The top is knitted from the top down.
(MAKE 1)
Cast on 24 sts in C.
Work 2 rows in st st beg with a k row.
Row 3: K6, m1, k1, m1, k10, m1, k1, m1, k to end. *(28 sts)*
Row 4: K2, p to last 2 sts, k2.
Row 5: K6, m1, k3, m1, k10, m1, k3, m1, k to end. *(32 sts)*
Row 6: K2, p to last 2 sts, k2.
Row 7: K6, m1, k5, m1, k10, m1, k5, m1, k to end. *(36 sts)*
Row 8: K2, p to last 2 sts, k2.
Row 9: K6, m1, k7, m1, k10, m1, k7, m1, k to end. *(40 sts)*
Row 10: K2, p5, bind (cast) off 7 sts kwise, (1 st rem on needle from binding/casting off), p11, bind (cast) off 7 sts kwise, (1 st rem on needle from binding/casting off), p4, k2. *(26 sts)*
Row 11: K7, turn, cast on 3 sts, turn, k12, turn, cast on 3 sts, turn, k to end. *(32 sts)*
Row 12: K2, p to last 2 sts, k2.
Row 13: K2, [m1, k2] to end. *(47 sts)*
Work 16 rows in st st beg with a p row.
Row 30: Knit.
Row 31: K2, [yo, k2tog] to last st, k1.
Row 32: Knit.
Bind (cast) off pwise.

TO MAKE UP TOP
Sew the back seam of the top, from the lower edge up to the base of the back opening worked in garter stitch. Using a yarn tail at the top of the left back, use the D3 (3.25mm) crochet hook to work a few crochet chains (see page 125). Secure the free end of the chain to form a button loop. Sew the green button to corresponding side. Weave in all loose ends.

pants

(MAKE 1)
Cast on 18 sts in D.
Row 1: Knit.
Leave D at side and join in E.
Work 2 rows in st st beg with a k row.
Leave E at side and use D.
Work 2 rows in st st beg with a k row.
Rep last 4 rows 5 times more.
Break yarns and leave sts on needle.
Cast on another 18 sts in D on needle with sts.
Leave D at side and join in E.
Work 2 rows in st st beg with a k row.
Leave E at side and use D.
Work 2 rows in st st beg with a k row.
Rep last 4 rows 5 times more but do not break yarn.
Now work across all 36 sts.
Work 12 rows in st st keeping to the striped patt and ending in 2 rows in D.
Break E and work rem of item in D.
Next row: [K1, p1] to end.
Rep last row 3 times more.
Bind (cast) off keeping to the k1, p1 patt.

TO MAKE UP PANTS
Sew inside leg and back seams.
Weave in all loose ends.

lab coat

BACK AND FRONT
(MAKE 1)
Cast on 48 sts in F.
Row 1: Knit.
Row 2: Knit.
Row 3: K2, p to last 2 sts, k2.
Rep rows 2–3, 11 times more.
Row 26: K10, k2tog, turn.
Work on these 11 sts only, leaving rem sts on needle. *(11 sts)*
Next row: P to last 2 sts, k2.
Next row: Knit.
Next row: P to last 2 sts, k2.
Rep last 2 rows twice more.
Next row: Knit.
Break yarn and rejoin it to rem 36 sts on RS of work.
Next row: Ssk, k20, k2tog, turn. *(22 sts)*

Work on these 22 sts only, leaving rem sts on needle.

Work 8 rows in st st beg with a p row. Break yarn and rejoin it to rem 12 sts on RS of work.

Next row: Ssk, k to end. *(11 sts)*
Next row: K2, p to end.
Next row: Knit.
Next row: K2, p to end.
Rep last 2 rows twice more.
Next row: Knit.
Now work across all 44 sts.
Next row: K2, p to last 2 sts, k2.
Next row: Bind (cast) off 2 sts pwise, (1 st rem on needle from binding/casting off), k6, ssk, k2tog, k2, ssk, k10, k2tog, k2, ssk, k2tog, k to end. *(36 sts)*
Next row: Bind (cast) off 2 sts, p to last st, k1. *(34 sts)*
Next row: K4, [ssk] twice, [k2tog] 3 times, k6, [ssk] 3 times, [k2tog] twice, k to end. *(24 sts)*
Knit 5 rows.
Bind (cast) off.

SLEEVES

(MAKE 2)
Cast on 17 sts in F.
Row 1: Knit.
Work 18 rows in st st beg with a k row.
Bind (cast) off.

POCKET

(MAKE 2)
Cast on 6 sts in F.
Row 1: Knit.
Work 4 rows in st st beg with a k row.
Bind (cast) off.

TO MAKE UP LAB COAT

Sew sleeve seams. Insert into armholes and stitch in place from the inside. Sew pale gray buttons onto coat using separated strand of F. The gaps between the knitted stitches can be used for buttonholes. Weave in all loose ends.

shoes

(MAKE 2)
Cast on 24 sts in G.
Work 4 rows in st st beg with a k row.
Row 5: K6, [ssk] 3 times, [k2tog] 3 times, k to end. *(18 sts)*
Row 6: Purl.
Row 7: K7, ssk, k2tog, k to end. *(16 sts)*
Bind (cast) off pwise.

STRAPS

(MAKE 2)
Cast on 10 sts in G.
Bind (cast) off.

TO MAKE UP SHOES

Fold shoe piece in half so that the right side is on the inside and oversew sole (see page 125). Turn the piece the right way out and sew the back seam. Sew short edge of strap to front of shoe on one side—remembering to make the shoes mirror images of each other. Secure the other short end with a bead. Weave in all loose ends.

safety goggles

Using D3 (3.25mm) crochet hook and yarn H, work a 5½-in (14-cm) crochet chain (see page 125). Sew the two yarn tails of the long chain to the center to create the eye frames. Weave in all loose ends. Thread a short length of the same yarn through each side of the goggles—these will be used to secure the goggles to the doll's face. Dip the goggles into a 50:50 solution of PVA glue and water, leaving the yarn at the sides free. Squeeze lightly. Shape and leave to dry thoroughly on a piece of waxed paper or similar. Spread a thin layer of undiluted PVA on the back of the eye part of the frame and place on the acetate. Leave to dry thoroughly. Trim the acetate to fit. Use the yarn at the sides to sew the goggles in place.

Bob the Baker

Whether it's a fondant fancy or a tray of chocolate brownies, Bob's always ready and willing to get baking. He wants to look the part, so loves his snow-white apron and matching cap. And if you want to knit him a gorgeous frosted cake, we've got that sorted, too!

YARN AND MATERIALS

Debbie Bliss Baby Cashmerino (55% wool, 33% acrylic, 12% cashmere), 137yd (125m) per 1¾oz (50g) ball of sport weight (light DK) yarn

- ¾ ball Camel 102 (A)—head and body, arms, legs
- ¼ ball Chocolate 11 (B)—hair
- ¼ ball Kingfisher 72 (C)—T-shirt, shoe soles, laces
- ¼ ball Orange 92 (D)—pants
- ½ ball Primrose 01 (E)—pants, cake
- ½ ball White 100 (F)—apron, hat, shoe uppers
- Very small amount of Black 300 (G)—eyes
- Small amount Baby Pink 601 (H)—cake frosting
- Very small amount of Red 34 (J)—cake filling

Very small amount of coral, red, or pink embroidery floss (thread) or yarn—mouth

⅜in (10mm) green button

6 x small red beads

1oz (30g) polyester toy filling

Small amount of toy filling for cake

NEEDLES AND EQUIPMENT

US3 (3.25mm) knitting needles

D3 (3.25mm) crochet hook (or one of similar size)

Yarn sewing needle

Large-eyed embroidery needle

2 stitch markers or small safety pins

Pins

Coloring pencil in deep pink or red

GAUGE (TENSION)

Approximately 25 stitches and 34 rows to 4in (10cm) over st st (see also page 14)

ABBREVIATIONS

See page 127

main doll

Work as for basic pattern on page 9. Work head and body pieces, arms and legs in A.

HAIR

(MAKE 1)
Cast on 18 sts in B.
Work 4 rows in st st beg with a k row.
Row 5: Ssk, k to last 2 sts, k2tog. (16 sts)
Row 6: Purl.
Rep last 2 rows twice more. (12 sts)
Row 11: Inc, k to last 2 sts, inc, k1. (14 sts)
Row 12: Purl.
Row 13: Inc, k4, k2tog, turn and work on 7 sts just worked, leaving rem sts on needle.
Next row: P2tog, p to end. (6 sts)
Next row: Inc, k3, k2tog.
Next row: P2tog, p to end. (5 sts)
Next row: K3, k2tog. (4 sts)
Next row: P2tog, p to end. (3 sts)
Next row: K1, k2tog. (2 sts)
Next row: P2tog. (1 st)
Fasten off.
Rejoin yarn to rem 7 sts on RS of work.
Next row: Ssk, k3, inc, k1.
Next row: P to last 2 sts, p2tog tbl. (6 sts)
Next row: Ssk, k2, inc, k1.
Next row: P to last 2 sts, p2tog tbl. (5 sts)
Next row: Ssk, k to end. (4 sts)

Next row: P2, p2tog tbl. (3 sts)
Next row: Ssk, k1. (2 sts)
Next row: P2tog. (1 st)
Fasten off.

TO MAKE UP DOLL

Make up main doll as explained on page 9.
For eyes, work French knots (see page 124) using G. Embroider mouth in straight stitch (see page 124) using embroidery floss (thread) or a separated strand of yarn. Work nose by working a couple of chain stitches (see page 124) in A, in a short vertical line. To make the nose slightly more prominent, work another couple of chain stitches over the ones you have just sewn. For the ears, work a few chain stitches in A in a short vertical line at the side of the head, in line with the eyes. Then work another row of chain stitches on top to make the ears a bit more prominent. Add a bit of color to the cheeks using the coloring pencil.
Seam the hair piece to form a cap shape. Pin then oversew (see page 125) the hair piece to the head, using matching yarn.
Weave in all loose ends.

polo shirt

The shirt is knitted from the top down.
(MAKE 1)
Cast on 24 sts in C.
Row 1: Knit.
Row 2: K6, m1, k1, m1, k10, m1, k1, m1, k to end. *(28 sts)*
Row 3: K2, p to last 2 sts, k2.
Row 4: K6, m1, k3, m1, k10, m1, k3, m1, k to end. *(32 sts)*
Row 5: K2, p to last 2 sts, k2.
Row 6: K6, m1, k5, m1, k10, m1, k5, m1, k to end. *(36 sts)*
Row 7: K2, p to last 2 sts, k2.
Row 8: K6, m1, k7, m1, k10, m1, k7, m1, k to end. *(40 sts)*
Row 9: K2, p5, bind (cast) off 7 sts kwise, (1 st rem on needle from binding/casting off), p11, bind (cast) off 7 sts kwise, (1 st rem on needle from binding/casting off), p4, k2. *(26 sts)*
Row 10: K7, turn, cast on 3 sts, turn, k12, turn, cast on 3 sts, turn, k to end. *(32 sts)*
Row 11: K2, p to last 2 sts, k2.
Work 13 rows in st st beg with a k row.
Knit 3 rows.
Bind (cast) off.

COLLAR

With RS facing and C, pick up and k 12 sts along cast-on edge, from center back to center front.
Knit 6 rows.
Bind (cast) off.
With RS facing, pick up and k another 12 sts from center front to center back.
Knit 6 rows.
Bind (cast) off.

TO MAKE UP SHIRT

Sew the back seam of the shirt, from the lower edge up to the base of the back opening worked in garter stitch. Using a yarn tail at the top of the left back below collar, use the crochet hook to work a few crochet chains (see page 125). Secure the free end of the chain to form a button loop. Sew button to corresponding side. Weave in all loose ends.

pants

(MAKE 1)
Cast on 17 sts in D.
Row 1: Knit.
Leave D at side and join in E.
Row 2: In E, [k1, sl1 pwise with yarn at back] to last st, k1.
Row 3: In E, [p1, sl1 pwise with yarn at front] to last st, p1.
Knit 2 rows in D.
Rep rows 2–5 (last 4 rows) 8 times more.
Rep rows 2–3 once more.
Break yarns and leave on needle.
Cast on 17 sts in D on empty needle.
Row 1: Knit.
Leave D at side and join in E.
Row 2: In E, [k1, sl1 pwise with yarn at back] to last st, k1.
Row 3: In E, [p1, sl1 pwise with yarn at front] to last st, p1.
Knit 2 rows in D.
Rep rows 2–5 (last 4 rows) 8 times more.
Rep rows 2–3 once more.
Now work across all 34 sts.
Next row: In D, k17, inc, k to end. *(35 sts)*
Next row: In D, knit.

Next row: In E, [k1, sl1 pwise with yarn at back] to last st, k1.
Next row: In E, [p1, sl1 pwise with yarn at front] to last st, p1.
Knit 2 rows in D.
Rep last 4 rows 3 times more.
Break E.
Next row: K1, [p1, k1] to end.
Next row: P1, [k1, p1] to end.
Bind (cast) off, keeping to k1, p1 patt.

TO MAKE UP PANTS

Sew inside leg and back seams.
Weave in all loose ends.

apron

The apron is worked from the top down.
(MAKE 1)
Cast on 10 sts in F leaving a 12in (30cm) yarn tail.
Row 1: K1, inc, k to last 2 sts, inc, k1. *(12 sts)*
Row 2: K2, p to last 2 sts, k2.
Row 3: Knit.
Row 4: K2, p to last 2 sts, k2.
Row 5: Knit.
Row 6: K2, p to last 2 sts, k2.

Rep rows 1–6 (last 6 rows) 5 times more. *(22 sts)*
Row 37: Knit.
Row 38: K2, p to last 2 sts, k2.
Rep rows 37–38 twice more.
Knit 2 rows.
Bind (cast) off.

POCKET
(MAKE 1)
Cast on 12 sts in F.
Row 1: Knit.
Work 9 rows in st st beg with a k row.
Bind (cast) off pwise.

NECK STRAP
Using crochet hook and yarn tail at top of apron, work a 3½-in (9-cm) chain (see page 125). Attach free end to the other side of apron top.

WAIST STRAP
(MAKE 2)
Using crochet hook and F, work two 6½-in (16.5-cm) chains (see page 125). Attach one end of each chain to waist part of apron. Weave remaining yarn tails into chain.

TO MAKE UP APRON
Weave in all loose ends.

baker's cap

BRIM
(MAKE 1)
Cast on 36 sts in F.
Knit 2 rows.
Work 6 rows in st st beg with a k row.
Bind (cast) off.

CROWN
(MAKE 1)
Cast on 8 sts in F.
Row 1: Inc, k to last 2 sts, inc, k1. *(10 sts)*
Row 2: Purl.
Rep rows 1–2 twice more. *(14 sts)*
Work 4 rows in st st beg with a k row.
Row 11: Ssk, k to last 2 sts, k2tog. *(12 sts)*
Row 12: Purl.
Rep rows 11–12 once more. *(10 sts)*
Row 15: Ssk, k to last 2 sts, k2tog.
Bind (cast) off pwise.

TO MAKE UP CAP
Sew the short sides of the brim to form a circle. Attach the crown of the cap to the brim from the inside.

shoes

(MAKE 2)
Cast on 26 sts in C.
Row 1: Knit.
Row 2: Purl.
Row 3: Knit.
Break C and join in F.
Work 4 rows in st st beg with a k row.
Row 8: K7, [ssk] 3 times, [k2tog] 3 times, k to end. *(20 sts)*
Row 9: Purl.
Row 10: K6, [ssk] twice, [k2tog] twice, k to end. *(16 sts)*
Row 11: Knit.
Bind (cast) off.

TO MAKE UP SHOES
Fold shoe pieces in half so that the right side is on the inside and oversew (see page 125) sole. Turn the pieces the right way out and sew the back seams. Using a separated strand of C, work two straight stitches (see page 124) on front of shoes to represent laces. Weave in all loose ends.

cake

TOP AND BASE
(MAKE 2)
Cast on 8 sts in E.
Row 1: Inc, k to last 2 sts, inc, k1. *(10 sts)*
Row 2: Purl.
Rep rows 1–2, 3 times more. *(16 sts)*
Work 2 rows in st st beg with a k row.
Mark beg and end of last row with a stitch marker or small safety pin.
Work 2 rows in st st beg with a k row.
Row 13: Ssk, k to last 2 sts, k2tog. *(14 sts)*
Row 14: Purl.
Rep rows 13–14 twice more. *(10 sts)*
Row 19: Ssk, k to last 2 sts, k2tog. *(8 sts)*
Bind (cast) off pwise.

SIDES
With RS of one piece of top/base facing and using E, pick up and knit 15 sts from one marker to the marker on the other side.
Work 5 rows in st st beg with a k row.
Bind (cast) off.
Rep for the other side.

FROSTING
(MAKE 1)
Cast on 36 sts in H.
Row 1: Knit.
Row 2: [P2tog] to end. *(18 sts)*
Row 3: Knit.
Row 4: [P2tog] to end. *(9 sts)*
Break yarn, thread through rem sts, and secure.

TO MAKE UP CAKE
Seam short edges of outer cake sides together. Join remaining top/base piece to sides, stuffing as you go. Sew frosting top in place using matching yarn. Using yarn J, work a row of chain stitch (see page 124) around the middle of the cake sides, using the photograph as a guide. Stitch red beads in place on frosting.

Rainbow Bella

Bella is in love with all things magical and sparkly, particularly unicorns. Her frilly-edged dress with its cute flower decoration is her top pick for everyday wear. And she's teamed it with not just a unicorn horn but also a striking pastel hair-do. Her pet rabbit is her friend of choice.

you will need

YARN AND MATERIALS

FOR DOLL

Debbie Bliss Baby Cashmerino (55% wool, 33% acrylic, 12% cashmere), 137yd (125m) per 1¾oz (50g) ball of sport weight (light DK) yarn
- ¾ ball Clotted Cream 65 (A)—head and body, arms
- ¼ ball Candy Pink 06 (B)—legs, hair, flower decoration
- ½ ball Primrose 01 (C)—hair, dress, flower decoration centers
- ¼ ball Baby Blue 204 (D)—hair
- ¼ ball Apple 02 (E)—hair, underpants, horn, flower decoration
- ¼ ball Speedwell 97 (F)—dress
- Very small amount of Lipstick Pink 78 (G)—horn
- Very small amount of Black 300 (H)—eyes
- Small amount Fuchsia 88 (J)—shoes

Very small amount of coral, red, or pink embroidery floss (thread) or yarn—mouth

⅜in (10mm) white button

3 x small silver star sequins

2 x small readymade silver bows

1oz (30g) polyester toy filling

FOR RABBIT

Debbie Bliss Baby Cashmerino (55% wool, 33% acrylic, 12% cashmere), 137yd (125m) per 1¾oz (50g) ball of sport weight (light DK) yarn
- ¼ ball Silver 12 (K)—main rabbit
- Small amount of White 100 (L)—pom-pom tail
- Very small amount of Black 300 (H)—features

Small amount of polyester toy filling

NEEDLES AND EQUIPMENT

US3 (3.25mm) knitting needles

D3 (3.25mm) crochet hook (or one of similar size)

J10 (6mm) crochet hook (or one of similar size)

Yarn sewing needle

Large-eyed embroidery needle

Pins

Coloring pencil in deep pink or red

GAUGE (TENSION)

Approximately 25 stitches and 34 rows to 4in (10cm) over st st (see also page 114)

ABBREVIATIONS

See page 127

main doll

Work as for basic pattern on page 9.
Work head and body pieces and arms
in A.
Work legs in B.

HAIR
(MAKE 1)
Cast on 18 sts in D.
Work 8 rows in st st beg with a k row.
Row 9: Ssk, k to last 2 sts, k2tog.
(16 sts)
Row 10: Purl.
Rep rows 9–10 twice more. *(12 sts)*
Row 15: Inc, k to last 2 sts, inc, k1.
(14 sts)
Row 16: Purl.
Row 17: Inc, k6, turn and work on
8 sts just worked, leaving rem sts
on needle.
Next row: Purl.
Next row: Inc, k5, ssk.
Next row: P2tog, p to end. *(7 sts)*
Next row: K to last 2 sts, ssk. *(6 sts)*
Rep last 2 rows once more. *(4 sts)*
Next row: P2tog, p to end. *(3 sts)*
Work 4 rows in st st beg with a k row.
Next row: K1, ssk. *(2 sts)*
Next row: P2tog. *(1 st)*
Fasten off.
Rejoin yarn to rem 7 sts on RS
of work.
Next row: K to last st, inc. *(8 sts)*
Next row: Purl.
Next row: K2tog, k to last st, inc.
Next row: P to last 2 sts, p2tog tbl.
(7 sts)
Next row: K2tog, k to end. *(6 sts)*
Rep last 2 rows once more. *(4 sts)*
Next row: P to last 2 sts, p2tog tbl.
(3 sts)
Work 4 rows in st st beg with a k row.
Next row: K2tog, k1. *(2 sts)*
Next row: P2tog tbl. *(1 st)*
Fasten off.
Cut 8 x 1½-yd (1.4-m) lengths of yarn
in each of B, C, D, and E. Using J10
(6mm) crochet hook and yarn
doubled, make 8 crochet chains
(see page 125), each measuring
about 3½in (9cm), for the rainbow
braids (plaits).

UNICORN HORN
(MAKE 1)
Cast on 6 sts in E.
Work 2 rows in st st beg with a k row.
Row 3: K2tog, k2, ssk. *(4 sts)*
Work 3 rows in st st beg with a k row.
Row 7: K2tog, ssk. *(2 sts)*
Row 8: P2tog. *(1 st)*
Fasten off.

TO MAKE UP DOLL
Make up main doll as explained on
page 9.
For eyes, work French knots (see page
124) using H. Using a single separated
strand of H, work straight stitches (see
page 124) for the eyelashes.
Embroider mouth in straight stitch
using embroidery floss (thread) or a
separated strand of yarn. Work nose
by working a couple of chain stitches
(see page 124) in A, in a short vertical
line. To make the nose slightly more
prominent, work another couple of
chain stitches over the ones you have
just sewn. Add a bit of color to the
cheeks using the coloring pencil. Sew
silver star sequins in place with a
single separated strand of A.
Seam the hair piece to form a cap
shape. Pin then oversew (see page
125) the hair piece to head, using
matching yarn, stitching the longer
front side parts into curls on the side

of the doll's face. Attach the braids
(plaits) to the sides of the head.
Dampen and shape if desired.
Seam the horn, stuff lightly, and attach
it to the forehead, using the
photograph as a guide. Using chain
stitch and a divided strand of G, work
a spiral from the bottom to the top of
the horn.
Weave in all loose ends.

dress

SKIRT
(MAKE 1)
Cast on 32 sts in F.
Leave F at side.
Row 1: In C, k1, [sl2 pwise with yarn
at back, k2] to last 3 sts, sl2 pwise
with yarn at back, k1.
Row 2: In C, k1, [sl2 pwise with yarn
at front, p2] to last 3 sts, sl2 pwise
with yarn at front, k1.
Row 3: In F, k1, [k2, sl2 pwise with
yarn at back] to last 3 sts, k3.
Row 4: In F, k1, [p2, sl2 pwise with
yarn at front] to last 3 sts, p2, k1.
Rep rows 1–4, 9 times more.
Break C.
Row 41: K1, [k2tog] to last st, k1.
(17 sts)
Bind (cast) off.

SKIRT EDGING

*Cast on 3 sts in F.
Bind (cast) off 2 sts.**
Transfer st from right-hand needle
to left-hand needle.
Rep from * to ** 25 times.

BODICE

The bodice is knitted from the
top down.
(MAKE 1)
Cast on 24 sts in F.
Row 1: Knit.
Break F and join in C.
Row 2: K6, m1, k1, m1, k10, m1, k1,
m1, k to end. *(28 sts)*
Row 3: K2, p to last 2 sts, k2.
Row 4: K6, m1, k3, m1, k10, m1, k3,
m1, k to end. *(32 sts)*
Row 5: K2, p to last 2 sts, k2.
Row 6: K6, m1, k5, m1, k10, m1, k5,
m1, k to end. *(36 sts)*
Row 7: K2, p to last 2 sts, k2.
Row 8: K6, m1, k7, m1, k10, m1, k7,
m1, k to end. *(40 sts)*
Row 9: K2, p5, bind (cast) off 7 sts
kwise, p11, (1 st rem on needle from
binding/casting off), bind (cast) off
7 sts kwise, (1 st rem on needle from
binding/casting off), p4, k2. *(26 sts)*
Row 10: K7, turn, cast on 3 sts, turn,
k12, turn, cast on 3 sts, turn, k to end.
(32 sts)
Row 11: K2, p to last 2 sts, k2.
Work 6 rows in st st beg with a k row.
Break C and join in F.
Row 18: Knit.
Bind (cast) off pwise.

FLOWER DECORATION

Make three flowers, one each in B, E,
and G.
Cast on 6 sts.
Bind (cast) off 2 sts.
*Transfer st from right-hand
to left-hand needle.
Cast on 2 sts.
Bind (cast) off 3 sts.**
Rep from * to ** twice more.
Fasten off.
To make flower shape, run your
yarn along the lower edge, pull up,
and secure.

TO MAKE UP DRESS

Sew the back seam of the bodice,
from the lower edge up to the base of
the back opening worked in garter
stitch. Using a yarn tail at the top of
the back of the bodice, use the D3
(3.25mm) crochet hook to work a few
crochet chains (see page 125). Secure
the free end of the chain to form a
button loop. Sew white button to
corresponding side. Sew the back
seam of the dress skirt. Join dress
bodice and skirt using mattress
stitch (see page 126). Slip stitch
skirt edging in place. Using C,
secure flowers in place with French
knots (see page 124) which will form
the flower centers.

underpants

(MAKE 1)
Cast on 16 sts in E.
Knit 2 rows.
Break yarn and cast on another 16 sts
on the same needle.
Knit 2 rows.
Now work across all 32 sts.
Work 8 rows in st st beg with a k row.
Next row: [K1, p1] to end.
Rep last row once more.
Bind (cast) off keeping to the k1,
p1 patt.

TO MAKE UP UNDERPANTS

Join inside leg and back seams.
Weave in all loose ends.

shoes

(MAKE 2)
Cast on 24 sts in J.
Row 1: Knit.
Row 2: Purl.
Row 3: Knit.
Work 4 rows in st st beg with a k row.
Row 8: K6, [ssk] 3 times, [k2tog]
3 times, k to end. *(18 sts)*
Bind (cast) off pwise.

TO MAKE UP SHOES
Fold shoe piece in half so that the
right side is on the inside and oversew
(see page 125) sole. Turn the piece the
right way out and sew the back seam.
Sew silver bows on the shoe fronts.
Weave in all loose ends.

rabbit

FACE
(MAKE 1)
Cast on 6 sts in K.
Row 1: Inc, k3, inc, k1. *(8 sts)*
Row 2: Purl.
Row 3: K1, m1, k to last st, m1, k1.
(10 sts)
Row 4: Purl.*
Row 5: K1, m1, k3, m1, k2, m1, k3,
m1, k1. *(14 sts)*
Row 6: Purl.
Row 7: K5, k2tog, ssk, k to end.
(12 sts)
Work 3 rows in st st beg with a p row.
Bind (cast) off.

HEAD BACK
(MAKE 1)
Work as for face to *.
Row 5: K1, m1, k to last st, m1, k1.
(12 sts)
Row 6: Purl.
Work 4 rows in st st beg with a k row.
Bind (cast) off.

BODY UPPER PART
(MAKE 1)
Cast on 5 sts in K.
Work 4 rows in st st.
Row 5: K1, m1, k to end. *(6 sts)*
Row 6: Purl.

Break yarn and leave sts on needle.
Cast on another 5 sts on needle
with sts.
Work 4 rows in st st.
Row 5: K to last st, m1, k1. *(6 sts)*
Row 6: Purl.
Work across all 12 sts.
Next row: K6, turn and cast on 4 sts,
turn back and k rem sts.* *(16 sts)*
Work 17 rows in st st beg with a
p row.
**Next row: K4, k2tog, bind (cast) off
4 sts, ssk (using st rem from binding/
casting off) as first slipped stitch, k to
end. *(2 groups of stitches with 5 sts
in each)*
Work on last group of 5 sts only,
leaving rem sts on needle.
Work 4 rows in st st beg with a p row.
Bind (cast) off pwise.
Rejoin yarn to rem 5 sts on WS
of work.
Work 4 rows in st st beg with a p row.
Bind (cast) off pwise.

GUSSET
(MAKE 1)
Using yarn K, work as for body upper
part from beg to *.
Next row: Purl.
Next row: Cast on 3 sts, k to end.
(19 sts)
Next row: Cast on 3 sts, p to end.
(22 sts)

Next row: Bind (cast) off 3 sts, k to end. *(19 sts)*
Next row: Bind (cast) off 3 sts, p to end. *(16 sts)*
Work as for body top from ** to end.

EARS
(MAKE 2)
Cast on 4 sts in K.
Work 4 rows in st st beg with a k row.
Row 5: Ssk, k2tog. *(2 sts)*
Row 6: P2tog. *(1 st)*
Fasten off.

POM-POM TAIL
(MAKE 1)
Wrap a length of yarn L round two fingers approx. 20 times. Slip yarn off fingers and tie in the middle. Trim edges then shape into a small pom-pom just over ¾in (2cm) in diameter.

TO MAKE UP RABBIT
Place two head pieces right sides together and oversew (see page 125) around outside, leaving the lower edge open for turning and stuffing. Turn, stuff lightly then close gap.
Place the body and gusset pieces right sides together and pin. The "peaks" on the gusset should reach up the main body piece to give the rabbit its shape under tail and chin. Oversew around the pieces, leaving a gap along one edge to turn and stuff. Turn, stuff lightly then close the gap.
Stitch pom-pom tail in place.
Using a divided length of H, work two French knots (see page 124) for the eyes. Work two straight stitches (see page 124) in a cross shape for the nose and mouth.
Weave in all loose ends.
You can gently brush the rabbit with a nylon toothbrush or nail brush to make it fluffier. Dampening the knitting before brushing it can make this easier.

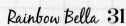

Finlay Fox

There's something a bit country estate about Finlay Fox, who loves his rural home. In his fashionable jacket with its asymmetrical front and mandarin collar, Finlay thinks of himself as a trendsetter among foxes. And, of course, there are those adorable green breeches that no self-respecting fox should be without.

you will need

YARN AND MATERIALS

Debbie Bliss Baby Cashmerino (55% wool, 33% acrylic, 12% cashmere), 137yd (125m) per 1¾oz (50g) ball of sport weight (light DK) yarn
- ¾ ball Sienna 67 (A)—main fox
- Small amount Ecru 101 (B)—main fox, eyes
- ½ ball Pale Lilac 608 (C)—jacket
- Small amount Drake 302 (D)—breeches
- ¼ ball Apple 02 (E)—breeches
- Very small amounts of Black 300 (F)—features

1oz (30g) polyester toy filling

4 x ⁵⁄₁₆in (8mm) white buttons

Small amount of purple sewing thread

NEEDLES AND EQUIPMENT

US3 (3.25mm) knitting needles

Yarn sewing needle

Large-eyed embroidery needle

GAUGE (TENSION)

Approximately 25 stitches and 34 rows to 4in (10cm) over st st (see also page 114)

ABBREVIATIONS

m1 below = Find the top loop of the stitch below the next stitch on the left-hand needle. Insert the tip of the right-hand needle into that top loop from front to back. If this is difficult try picking up the stitch from the back, hold it with the left thumb and forefinger, then remove the needle and reinsert it into the loop from front to back. Knit into the stitch then knit into the stitch on the needle (see page 121).

See also page 127

body and head

FRONT
(MAKE 1)
Cast on 18 sts in A.
Work 28 rows in st st beg with a k row.
Row 29: [Ssk] 4 times, k2, [k2tog] 4 times. *(10 sts)*

Work 3 rows in st st beg with a p row.
Break A and join in B.
Row 33: K1, m1 below, k to last 2 sts, m1 below, k1. *(12 sts)*
Row 34: Purl.
Rep rows 33–34 twice more.* *(16 sts)*
Row 39: K1, m1 below, k6, m1, k6, m1 below, k1. *(19 sts)*
Row 40: Purl.

Row 41: In B, k1, ssk, k6, m1; join in A and k1; with B from ball center: m1, k6, k2tog, k1.
Row 42: P8 in B, 3 in A, 8 in B.
Row 43: In B, k1, ssk, k5; in A, m1, k3, m1; in B, k5, k2tog, k1.
Row 44: P7 in B, 5 in A, 7 in B. Break all yarns and rejoin A to RS of work.
Row 45: K1, ssk, k4, m1, k5, m1, k4, k2tog, k1.
Row 46: Purl.
Row 47: K1, ssk, k3, m1, k7, m1, k3, k2tog, k1.
Row 48: Purl.
Row 49: K1, ssk, k2, m1, k9, m1, k2, k2tog, k1.
Row 50: Purl.
Row 51: Knit.
Row 52: Purl.
Row 53: K1, ssk, k to last 3 sts, k2tog, k1. *(17 sts)*
Bind (cast) off pwise.

BACK

(MAKE 1)
Work as for front to *.
Row 39: K1, m1 below, k to last 2 sts, m1 below, k1. *(18 sts)*
Work 13 rows in st st beg with a p row.
Row 53: K1, ssk, k to last 3 sts, k2tog, k1. *(16 sts)*
Bind (cast) off pwise.

ARMS

(MAKE 2)
Cast on 11 sts in A.
Work 32 rows in st st beg with a k row.
Row 33: K1, ssk, k5, k2tog, k1. *(9 sts)*
Break yarn and thread it through rem sts.

LEGS

(MAKE 2)
Cast on 30 sts in A.
Work 4 rows in st st beg with a k row.
Row 5: K9, [ssk] 3 times, [k2tog] 3 times, k to end. *(24 sts)*
Row 6: Purl.
Row 7: K6, [ssk] 3 times, [k2tog] 3 times, k to end. *(18 sts)*
Row 8: Purl.
Row 9: K5, [ssk] twice, [k2tog] twice, k to end. *(14 sts)*
Row 10: Purl.
Row 11: K5, ssk, k2tog, k to end. *(12 sts)*
Work 27 rows in st st beg with a p row.
Bind (cast) off.

EARS

(MAKE 4)
Cast on 8 sts in A.
Work 4 rows in st st beg with a k row.
Row 5: K1, ssk, k2, k2tog, k1. *(6 sts)*
Row 6: Purl.
Row 7: K1, ssk, k2tog, k1. *(4 sts)*
Row 8: P2tog, p2tog tbl. *(2 sts)*
Row 9: K2tog. *(1 st)*

TO MAKE UP FOX

Make up main animal in the same way as basic doll explained on page 9. For the ears, work Swiss embroidery (see page 125) in B (see chart, opposite) on two ear pieces to form ear fronts. Seam each front to a back piece along sides and lower edge using mattress stitch (see page 126). Sew in position using the photograph as a guide.
For eyes, work French knots (see page 124) using F. Using B, work a circle of chain stitch (see page 124) around each French knot. For nose, work a small coil of chain stitches using F. Add a straight vertical stitch at the bottom using a separated strand of the same yarn. You can gently brush the head with a nylon toothbrush or nail brush to make it fluffier. Dampening the knitting before brushing it can make this easier.

jacket

BACK AND FRONT

(MAKE 1)
Cast on 44 sts in C.
Knit 2 rows.
Row 3: K2, p to last 2 sts, k2.
Row 4: Knit.
Row 5: K2, p to last 2 sts, k2.
Row 6: K to last 2 sts, m1 below, k1. *(45 sts)*
Row 7: K2, p to last 2 sts, k2.
Rep rows 4–7 (last 4 rows) once more. *(46 sts)*
Row 12: Knit.
Row 13: K2, p to last 2 sts, k2.
Row 14: K11, turn.
Work on these 11 sts only leaving rem sts on needle.
Next row: P to last 2 sts, k2.
Next row: Knit.
Next row: P to last 2 sts, k2.
Rep last 2 rows twice more.
Next row: Knit.
Break yarn and rejoin it to rem 35 sts on RS of work.
Next row: K22, turn.
Work on these 22 sts only leaving rem sts on needle.
Work 8 rows in st st beg with a p row.
Break yarn and rejoin it to rem 13 sts on RS of work.
Next row: K to last 2 sts, m1 below, k1. *(14 sts)*
Next row: K2, p to last 2 sts, k2.
Next row: Knit.
Next row: K2, p to last 2 sts, k2.
Rep last 4 rows once more. *(15 sts)*
Next row: K to last 2 sts, m1 below, k1. *(16 sts)*
Now work across all 49 sts.
Next row: K2, p to last 2 sts, k2.
Next row: K4, ssk, k2, ssk, k2, k2tog, k2, k2tog, k2, k2tog, ssk, k2, ssk, k2, ssk, k2, k2tog, k2, k2tog, k to end. *(39 sts)*
Next row: K8, ssk, k2, ssk, k2tog, k2, k2tog, k4, ssk, k2, ssk, k2tog, k2, k2tog, k to end. *(31 sts)*
Next row: Knit.
Next row: Bind (cast) off 5 sts, k to end. *(26 sts)*
Knit 2 rows.
Bind (cast) off.

SLEEVES

(MAKE 2)

Cast on 16 sts in C.

Row 1: Knit.

Work 20 rows in st st beg with a
k row.

Bind (cast) off.

TO MAKE UP JACKET

Sew sleeve seams. Insert into
armholes and stitch in place from the
inside. Sew buttons onto jacket using
purple sewing thread. The gaps
between the knitted stitches can be
used for buttonholes. Weave in all
loose ends.

breeches

(MAKE 1)

Cast on 11 sts in D.

*Knit 4 rows.

Break D and join in E.

Row 4: [Inc pwise] to end. *(22 sts)*

Work 12 rows in st st beg with a
k row. **

Break yarn.

Cast on another 11 sts in D on
empty needle.

Rep from * to ** but do not break yarn.

Now work across all 44 sts.

Work 10 rows in st st beg with a
k row.

Next row: K3, [k2tog, k3] twice,
[ssk, k3] twice, k1, [k2tog, k3] twice,
[ssk, k3] twice. *(36 sts)*

Next row: [K1, p1] to end.

Rep last row 3 times more.

Bind (cast) off keeping to the k1,
p1 patt.

TO MAKE UP BREECHES

Sew inside leg and back seams.
Weave in all loose ends.

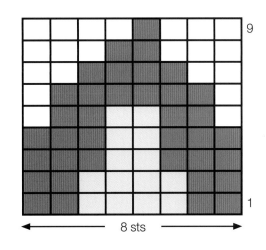

■ Sienna 67
☐ Ecru 101

9

1

8 sts

Ballerina Caterina

Whether it's a pirouette, a plié, or even a grand jeté, it's sure to be in Caterina's repertoire. Pretty, poised, and confident in her gorgeous lacy dress, she's always ready for the next challenging role. And she's got a wrap cardigan to hand in case the rehearsal room turns chilly.

you will need

YARN AND MATERIALS

Debbie Bliss Baby Cashmerino (55% wool, 33% acrylic, 12% cashmere), 137yd (125m) per 1¾oz (50g) ball of sport weight (light DK) yarn

- ½ ball of Camel 102 (A)—head and body, arms
- ¼ ball of Ecru 101 (B)—legs
- ¼ ball of Black 300 (C)—hair and eyes
- ½ ball of Baby Pink 601 (D)—dress
- ¼ ball of Speedwell 97 (E)—wrap cardigan
- Small amount of Silver 12 (F) —underpants
- Small amount of Lipstick Pink 78 (G)—shoes

Very small amount of coral, red, or pink embroidery floss (thread) or yarn—mouth

24 x 3½in (60 x 9cm) piece of white net fabric or organza

8-in (20-cm) length of thin elastic or elastic cord in white

¾in (2cm) readymade organza bow in pale pink

2 x ³⁄₁₆in (4mm) pearl beads

Small fabric flower

1oz (30g) polyester toy filling

NEEDLES AND EQUIPMENT

US3 (3.25mm) knitting needles

D3 (3.25mm) crochet hook (or one of similar size)

Yarn sewing needle

Large-eyed embroidery needle

Pins

Coloring pencil in deep pink or red

GAUGE (TENSION)

Approximately 25 stitches and 34 rows to 4in (10cm) over st st (see also page 114)

ABBREVIATIONS

See page 127

main doll

Work as for basic pattern on page 9.
Work head and body pieces and arms in A.
Work legs in B.

HAIR MAIN PIECE

(MAKE 1)

Cast on 18 sts in C.

Work 4 rows in st st beg with a k row.

Row 5: Ssk, k to last 2 sts, k2tog. *(16 sts)*

Row 6: Purl.

Rep last 2 rows twice more. *(12 sts)*

Row 11: Inc, k to last 2 sts, inc, k1. *(14 sts)*

Row 12: Purl.

Row 13: Inc, k4, k2tog, turn and work on 7 sts just worked, leaving rem sts on needle.

Next row: P2tog, p to end. *(6 sts)*

Next row: Inc, k3, k2tog.

Next row: P2tog, p to end. *(5 sts)*

Next row: K3, k2tog. *(4 sts)*

Next row: P2tog, p2. *(3 sts)*

Next row: K1, k2tog. *(2 sts)*

Next row: P2tog. *(1 st)*

Fasten off.

Rejoin yarn to rem 7 sts on RS of work.

Next row: Ssk, k3, inc, k1.

Next row: P to last 2 sts, p2tog tbl. *(6 sts)*

Next row: Ssk, k2, inc, k1.

Next row: P to last 2 sts, p2tog tbl. *(5 sts)*

Next row: Ssk k to end. *(4 sts)*
Next row: P2, p2tog tbl. *(3 sts)*
Next row: Ssk, k1. *(2 sts)*
Next row: P2tog. *(1 st)*
Fasten off.

BUN
(MAKE 1)
Cast on 4 sts in C.
Row 1: [Inc] 4 times. *(8 sts)*
Row 2: Purl.
Row 3: [Inc] 8 times. *(16 sts)*
Work 3 rows in st st beg with a p row.
Row 7: [K2tog] 8 times. *(8 sts)*
Row 8: [P2tog] 4 times. *(4 sts)*
Break yarn and thread through rem sts.

TO MAKE UP DOLL
Make up main doll as explained on page 9. For eyes, work French knots (see page 124) using C. Embroider mouth in straight stitch (see page 124) using embroidery floss (thread) or a separated strand of yarn. Work nose by working a couple of chain stitches (see page 124) in A, in a short vertical line. To make the nose slightly more prominent, work another couple of chain stitches over the ones you have just sewn. For the ears, work a few chain stitches in A, in a short vertical line at the side of the head, in line with the eyes. Then work another row of chain stitches on top to make the ears a bit more prominent. Stitch beads in place for earrings, using the photograph as a guide. Add a bit of color to the cheeks using the coloring pencil.
Seam the hair piece to form a cap shape. Pin then oversew (see page 125) the hair piece to head, using matching yarn. For bun, run yarn tail around the outside of the knitted pieces, very close to the edge. Pull up into a small sphere shape, stuffing with a small piece of filling as you go. Stitch in place on top of the head. Stitch fabric flower in place on front of bun.
Weave in all loose ends.

dress

BODICE FRONT
(MAKE 1)
Cast on 17 sts in D.
Row 1: K1, [p1, k1] to end.
Rep row 1, 11 times more.
Row 13: Bind (cast) off 3 sts keeping to patt, (1 st rem on needle from binding/casting off), k1, p1, bind (cast) off 3 sts keeping to patt, (1 st rem on needle from binding/casting off), k1, p1, bind (cast) off rem sts keeping to patt.
Rejoin yarn to 3 sts on needle on WS of work.
*Next row: P1, k1, p1.
Rep last row 20 times more.
Bind (cast) off keeping to patt.**
Rejoin yarn to rem 3 sts on needle on WS of work.
Rep from * to **.

BODICE BACK
(MAKE 1)
Cast on 17 sts in D.
Row 1: K1, [p1, k1] to end.
Rep row 1, 11 times more.
Row 13: Bind (cast) off keeping to patt.

SKIRT
(MAKE 1)
Cast on 58 sts in D.
Row 1: Knit.
Row 2: K2, [k2tog, yo, k1, yo, k1, sl1, psso, k2] to end.
Row 3: Purl.

Row 4: K1, [k2tog, yo, k3, yo, sl1, k1, psso] to last st, k1.
Row 5: Purl.
Rep rows 2–5, 5 times more.
Row 26: K1, [k2tog] to last st, k1. *(30 sts)*
Bind (cast) off.

UNDERSKIRT

Fold down ¾in (2cm) along one of the long edges of the net fabric. Thread elastic in and out of fabric along this edge, about ⅜in (1cm) down from top. Gather to fit doll's waist and tie or sew elastic to secure.

TO MAKE UP DRESS

Join bodice sides and sew short edges of straps in place on bodice back. Slip stitch skirt to bodice, matching back seams. Weave in all loose ends. Stitch organza bow in place on bodice front.

wrap cardigan

FRONT AND BACK

(MAKE 1)
Cast on 46 sts in E, leaving long (23½in/60cm) yarn tail.
Row 1: Knit.
Row 2: K1, ssk, k to last 3 sts, k2tog, k1. *(44 sts)*
Row 3: K2, p to last 2 sts, k2.
Rep rows 2–3, 6 times more. *(32 sts)*
Row 16: K1, ssk, k4, turn.
Work on 6 sts just worked only, leaving rem sts on needle.
Next row: P4, k2.
Next row: K1, ssk, k3. *(5 sts)*
Next row: P3, k2.
Next row: K1, ssk, k2. *(4 sts)*
Next row: P2, k2.
Next row: K1, ssk, k1. *(3 sts)*
Break yarn and rejoin it to rem sts on RS of work.
Next row: K18, turn.
Work on 18 sts just worked only, leaving rem sts on needle.
Next row: Purl.
Next row: K2, ssk, k to last 4 sts, k2tog, k2. *(16 sts)*
Work 3 rows in st st beg with a p row.

Next row: K2, ssk, k to last 4 sts, k2tog, k2. *(14 sts)*
Break yarn and rejoin it to 7 rem sts on RS of work.
Next row: K4, k2tog, k1. *(6 sts)*
Next row: K2, p4.
Next row: K3, k2tog, k1. *(5 sts)*
Next row: K2, p3.
Next row: K2, k2tog, k1. *(4 sts)*
Next row: K2, p2.
Next row: K1, k2tog, k1. *(3 sts)*
Now work across all 20 sts on needle.
Next row: Knit.
Bind (cast) off.

SLEEVES

(MAKE 2)
Cast on 16 sts in E.
Work 20 rows in st st beg with a k row.
Bind (cast) off.

TO MAKE UP CARDIGAN

Join sleeve seams. Insert sleeves into armholes and stitch in place from the inside. Using crochet hook and long yarn tail from casting on, make a 7-in (18-cm) crochet chain (see page 125). Make a matching chain for other side of cardigan and stitch in place. Weave in all loose ends.

underpants

(MAKE 1)
Cast on 16 sts in F.
Knit 2 rows.
Break yarn and cast on another 16 sts on the same needle.
Knit 2 rows.
Now knit across all 32 sts.
Work 8 rows in st st beg with a k row.
Next row: [K1, p1] to end.
Rep last row once more.
Bind (cast) off keeping to the k1, p1 patt.

TO MAKE UP UNDERPANTS

Join inside leg and back seams. Weave in all loose ends.

shoes

(MAKE 2)
Cast on 24 sts in G.
Work 4 rows in st st beg with a k row.
Row 5: K6, [ssk] 3 times, [k2tog] 3 times, k to end. *(18 sts)*
Bind (cast) off pwise.

For ribbon ties, use crochet hook and four divided 1-yd (91-cm) lengths of G to work four 9-in (23-cm) chains (see page 125).

TO MAKE UP SHOES

Fold shoe piece in half so that the right side is on the inside and oversew (see page 125) sole. Turn the piece the right way out and sew the back seam. Attach ribbon ties to sides of shoes using the photograph as a guide. Weave in all loose ends.

Mermaid Marion

When she's not swimming in the sea, Marion loves to sit on a rock and style her shining auburn hair. Mermaids are some of the most enchanting and popular characters in books of all types, and we hope Mermaid Marion will be one of the favorite dolls in this one!

you will need

YARN AND MATERIALS
Debbie Bliss Baby Cashmerino (55% wool, 33% acrylic, 12% cashmere), 137yd (125m) per 1¾oz (50g) ball of sport weight (light DK) yarn
- ½ ball of Clotted Cream 65 (A)—head and body, arms
- ¼ ball of Sienna 67 (B)—hair
- ½ ball of Duck Egg 26 (C)—tail and bra top
- Very small amount of Black 300—eyes

Very small amount of coral, red, or pink embroidery floss (thread) or yarn—mouth

7-in (18-cm) length of ¼-in (7-mm) ribbon in gold

1oz (30g) polyester toy filling

NEEDLES AND EQUIPMENT
US3 (3.25mm) knitting needles

D3 (3.25mm) crochet hook (or one of similar size)

J10 (6mm) crochet hook (or one of similar size)

Yarn sewing needle

Large-eyed embroidery needle

Pins

Coloring pencil in deep pink or red

GAUGE (TENSION)
Approximately 25 stitches and 34 rows to 4in (10cm) over st st (see also page 114)

ABBREVIATIONS
m1 below = Find the top loop of the stitch below the next stitch on the left-hand needle. Insert the tip of the right-hand needle into that top loop from front to back. If this is difficult try picking up the stitch from the back, hold it with the left thumb and forefinger, then remove the needle and reinsert it into the loop from front to back. Knit into the stitch then knit into the stitch on the needle (see page 121).

See also page 127

main doll

Work arms in A as in basic pattern on page 9.

BODY AND HEAD
(MAKE 2)
Cast on 18 sts in A.
Work 16 rows in st st beg with a k row.
Row 17: [Ssk] 4 times, k2, [k2tog] 4 times. (10 sts)
Row 18: P2tog, p to last 2 sts, p2tog tbl. (8 sts)
Work 2 rows in st st beg with a k row.
Row 21: K1, [m1 below] twice, k2, [m1 below] twice, k1. (12 sts)
Row 22: Purl.
Row 23: K1, [m1 below] twice, k6, [m1 below] twice, k1. (16 sts)
Row 24: Purl.
Row 25: K1, [m1 below], k12, [m1 below], k1. (18 sts)
Work 13 rows in st st beg with a p row.
Row 39: K1, ssk, k to last 3 sts, k2tog, k1. (16 sts)
Row 40: Purl.
Rep rows 39–40 once more. (14 sts)
Row 43: K2, ssk, k6, k2tog, k2. (12 sts)
Bind (cast) off pwise.

HAIR

(MAKE 1)

Cast on 18 sts in B.

Work 4 rows in st st beg with a k row.

Row 5: Ssk, k to last 2 sts, k2tog. *(16 sts)*

Row 6: Purl.

Rep last 2 rows twice more. *(12 sts)*

Row 11: Inc, k to last 2 sts, inc, k1. *(14 sts)*

Row 12: Purl.

Row 13: Inc, k4, k2tog, turn and work on 7 sts just worked, leaving rem sts on needle.

Next row: P2tog, p to end. *(6 sts)*

Next row: Inc, k3, k2tog.

Next row: P2tog, p to end. *(5 sts)*

Next row: K3, k2tog. *(4 sts)*

Next row: P2tog, p to end. *(3 sts)*

Next row: K1, k2tog. *(2 sts)*

Next row: P2tog. *(1 st)*

Fasten off.

Rejoin yarn to rem 7 sts on RS of work.

Next row: Ssk, k3, inc, k1.

Next row: P to last 2 sts, p2tog tbl. *(6 sts)*

Next row: Ssk, k2, inc, k1.

Next row: P to last 2 sts, p2tog tbl. *(5 sts)*

Next row: Ssk, k to end. *(4 sts)*

Next row: P to last 2 sts, p2tog tbl. *(3 sts)*

Next row: Ssk, k1. *(2 sts)*

Next row: P2tog. *(1 st)*

Fasten off.

BRAID (PLAIT)

(MAKE 1)

Using J10 (6mm) crochet hook and four 1-yd (91-cm) lengths of B together, work a 6-in (15-cm) crochet chain (see page 125). Fasten off leaving long ends.

TAIL

The tail is worked from the waist down.

(MAKE 2)

Cast on 18 sts in C.

Knit 2 rows.

Row 3: [K3, m1] twice, k6, [m1, k3] twice. *(22 sts)*

Row 4: [P2, k3] to last 2 sts, p2.

Row 5: [K2, p3] to last 2 sts, k2.

Row 6: [P2, yb, sl1, k2, psso] to last 2 sts, p2. *(18 sts)*

Row 7: [K2, p1, yo, p1] to last 2 sts, k2. *(22 sts)*

Rep rows 4–7 (last 4 rows) 3 times.

Row 20: P2, [k3, p2tog] 3 times, k3, p2. *(19 sts)*

Row 21: K2, [p3, k1] 3 times, p3, k2.

Row 22: P2, [yb, sl1, k2, psso, p1] 4 times, p1. *(15 sts)*

Row 23: K2, [p1, yo, p1, k1] 4 times, k1. *(19 sts)*

Row 24: P2, [k3, p1] 4 times, p1.

Rep rows 21–24 once more.

Rep rows 21–23 once more.

Row 32: P2tog, [k3, p1] 3 times, k3, p2tog. *(17 sts)*

Row 33: K1, [p3, k1] to end.

Row 34: P1, [yb, sl1, k2, psso, p1] to end. *(13 sts)*

Row 35: [K1, p1, yo, p1] to last st, k1. *(17 sts)*

Row 36: P1, [k3, p1] to end.

Row 37: K1, [p3, k1] to end.

Row 38: P1, yb, sl1, k2tog, psso, [p1, yb, sl1, k2, psso] twice, p1, yb, sl1,

k2tog, psso, p1. *(11 sts)*
Row 39: K1, p1, k1, [p1, yo, p1, k1] twice, p1, k1. *(13 sts)*
Row 40: P1, k1, p1, [k3, p1] twice, k1, p1.
Row 41: P2tog, [k1, p3] twice, k1, p2tog tbl. *(11 sts)*
Row 42: K1, m1, k4, inc, k4, m1, k1. *(14 sts)*
Divide for tail
Row 43: P7, turn and work on these 7 sts only, leaving rem sts on needle.
Next row: K to last st, m1, k1. *(8 sts)*
Next row: Purl.
Rep last 2 rows once more. *(9 sts)*
Next row: K1, ssk, k5, m1, k1.
Next row: Purl.
Next row: K1, ssk, k3, k2tog, k1. *(7 sts)*
Next row: P2tog, p3, p2tog tbl. *(5 sts)*
Next row: Ssk, k1, k2tog. *(3 sts)*
Next row: P3tog. *(1 st)*
Break yarn and join to rem 7 sts on WS of work.
Next row: Purl.
Next row: K1, m1, k to end. *(8 sts)*
Next row: Purl.
Rep last 2 rows once more. *(9 sts)*
Next row: K1, m1, k to last 3 sts, k2tog, k1.
Next row: Purl.
Next row: K1, m1, k5, k2tog, k1.
Next row: Purl.
Next row: K1, ssk, k3, k2tog, k1. *(7 sts)*
Next row: P2tog, p3, p2tog tbl. *(5 sts)*
Next row: Ssk, k1, k2tog. *(3 sts)*
Next row: P3tog. *(1 st)*
Fasten off.

TO MAKE UP DOLL

Make up upper part of doll as explained on page 9. Sew side seams of tail, stuff and stitch to main body. For eyes, work French knots (see page 124) using black yarn. Embroider mouth in straight stitch (see page 124) using embroidery floss (thread) or a separated strand of yarn. Work nose by working a couple of chain stitches (see page 124) in A, in a short vertical line. To make the nose slightly more prominent, work another couple of chain stitches over the ones you have just sewn. For the ears, work a few chain stitches in A, in a short vertical line at the side of the head, in line with the eyes. Then work another row of chain stitches on top to make the ears a bit more prominent. For belly button, work a stitch from the back to the front of the doll and pull slightly before securing. Add a bit of color to the cheeks using the coloring pencil. Seam the hair piece to form a cap shape. Pin then oversew (see page 125) the hair piece to head, using matching yarn. Sew one end of the crochet chain in place on top of the head. Weave in all loose ends. Tie the ribbon around the end of the braid, trim, and separate strands of yarn at end of braid (plait).

bra top

(MAKE 1)
Cast on 32 sts in C.
Row 1: Knit.
Row 2: Purl.
Row 3: K4, *[m1, k1] 4 times, [skpo] twice, [k2tog] twice, rep from * to end once more, k to end.
Row 4: Purl.
Row 5: K4, *k4, [skpo] twice, [k2tog] twice, rep from * once more, k to end. *(24 sts)*
Row 6: Knit.
Bind (cast) off.

STRAPS

(MAKE 2)
Using D3 (3.25mm) crochet hook and C, work two crochet chains (see page 125) each measuring just under 1½in (3.5cm) long.

TO MAKE UP BRA TOP

Sew back seam of top. Sew straps in place on back and front of top. Weave in all loose ends.

Bedtime Billy

Billy works hard and plays hard. But every night when the clock strikes nine, he's yawning and ready for the Land of Nod. So he puts on his pale blue pajamas and picks up his teddy, George. Anyone for a nice mug of cocoa, a good book, and a cuddle?

you will need

YARN AND MATERIALS

Debbie Bliss Baby Cashmerino (55% wool, 33% acrylic, 12% cashmere), 137yd (125m) per 1¾oz (50g) ball of sport weight (light DK) yarn
  ¾ ball of Camel 102 (A)—head and body, arms, legs
  ¼ ball of Black 300 (B)—hair and eyes
  ¾ ball of Baby Blue 204 (C)—pajamas
  Small amount of Primrose 01 (D)—little teddy

Very small amount of coral, red, or pink embroidery floss (thread) or yarn—mouth

3 x ⅜in (10mm) white buttons

6-in (15-cm) length of very narrow (⅛in/3mm) red ribbon

1oz (30g) polyester toy filling

Small amount of polyester toy filling for teddy

NEEDLES AND EQUIPMENT

US3 (3.25mm) knitting needles

D3 (3.25mm) crochet hook (or one of similar size)

Yarn sewing needle

Large-eyed embroidery needle

Pins

Coloring pencil in deep pink or red

GAUGE (TENSION)

Approximately 25 stitches and 34 rows to 4in (10cm) over st st (see also page 114)

ABBREVIATIONS

m1 below = Find the top loop of the stitch below the next stitch on the left-hand needle. Insert the tip of the right-hand needle into that top loop from front to back. If this is difficult try picking up the stitch from the back, hold it with the left thumb and forefinger, then remove the needle and reinsert it into the loop from front to back. Knit into the stitch then knit into the stitch on the needle (see page 121).

See also page 127

main doll

Work as for basic pattern on page 9. Work head and body pieces, arms and legs in A.

HAIR
(MAKE 1)
Cast on 18 sts in B.
Work 4 rows in st st beg with a k row.
Row 5: Ssk, k to last 2 sts, k2tog. *(16 sts)*
Row 6: Purl.
Rep last 2 rows twice more. *(12 sts)*
Row 11: Inc, k7, turn. *(9 sts)*
Next row: P2tog, p to end, turn. *(8 sts)*
Next row: Inc, k5, k2tog, turn.
Next row: P2tog, p to end, turn. *(7 sts)*
Next row: Inc, k4, k2tog, turn.
Next row: P2tog, p to end, turn. *(6 sts)*
Next row: K4, k2tog, turn. *(5 sts)*
Next row: P2tog, p to end, turn. *(4 sts)*
Next row: K2, k2tog, turn. *(3 sts)*
Next row: P2tog, p1. *(2 sts)*
Next row: K2tog. *(1 st)*
Fasten off.
Rejoin yarn to rem 4 sts on RS of work.
Next row: K to last st, inc. *(5 sts)*
Next row: Purl.
Rep last 2 rows once more. *(6 sts)*
Next row: Ssk, k to last st, inc.
Next row: Purl.

Next row: Ssk, k to end. *(5 sts)*
Next row: P to last 2 sts, p2tog.
(4 sts)
Rep last 2 rows once more. *(2 sts)*
Next row: K2tog. *(1 st)*
Fasten off.

TO MAKE UP DOLL
Make up main doll as explained on page 9. For eyes, work French knots (see page 124) wrapping the yarn around once instead of the normal twice, then work a straight stitch (see page 124) across the top using B. Embroider mouth in straight stitch using embroidery floss (thread) or a separated strand of yarn. Work nose by working a couple of chain stitches (see page 124) in A, in a short vertical line. To make the nose slightly more prominent, work another couple of chain stitches over the ones you have just sewn. For the ears, work a few chain stitches in A, in a short vertical line at the side of the head, in line with the eyes. Then work another row of chain stitches on top to make the ears a bit more prominent. Add a bit of color to the cheeks using the coloring pencil.
Seam the hair piece to form a cap shape. Pin then oversew (see page 125) the hair piece to head, using matching yarn.
Weave in all loose ends.

pajamas

JACKET
(MAKE 1)
Cast on 43 sts in C.
Row 1: K1, [p1, k1] to end.
Rep row 1 twice more.
Row 4: K1, p1, k1, p to last 3 sts, k1, p1, k1.
Row 5: K1, p1, k to last 2 sts, p1, k1.
Row 6: K1, p1, k1, p to last 3 sts, k1, p1, k1.
Rep rows 5–6, 7 times more.
Row 21: K1, p1, k9, turn.
Work on these 11 sts only, leaving rem sts on needle.
Next row: P to last 3 sts, k1, p1, k1.
Next row: K1, p1, k to end.
Rep last 2 rows, 3 times more.

Break yarn and rejoin it to rem sts on RS of work.
Next row: K21, turn.
Work on these 21 sts only, leaving rem sts on needle.
Work 8 rows in st st beg with a p row.
Break yarn and rejoin it to rem 11 sts on RS of work.
Next row: K to last 2 sts, p1, k1.
Next row: K1, p1, k1, p to end.
Rep last 2 rows, 3 times more.
Next row: K to last 2 sts, p1, k1.
Now work across all 43 sts.
Next row: K1, p1, k1, p to last 3 sts, k1, p1, k1.
Next row: Bind (cast) off 2 sts (1 st rem on needle from binding/casting off), k6, ssk, k2tog, k2, ssk, k9, k2tog, k2, ssk, k2tog, k to last 2 sts, p1, k1. *(35 sts)*

Next row: Bind (cast) off 2 sts pwise, p to end. *(33 sts)*
Next row: K4, [ssk] twice, [k2tog] 3 times, k5, [ssk] 3 times, [k2tog] twice, k to end. *(23 sts)*
Next row: K1, [p1, k1] to end.
Rep last row 5 times more.
Bind (cast) off.

SLEEVES
(MAKE 2)
Cast on 17 sts in C.
Row 1: K1, [p1, k1] to end.
Rep row 1 twice more.
Work 16 rows in st st beg with a k row.
Bind (cast) off.

PANTS

(MAKE 1)

Cast on 17 sts in C.

Row 1: K1, [p1, k1] to end.

Rep row 1 twice more.

Work 22 rows in st st beg with a k row.

Break yarn and leave sts on needle.

Cast on 17 sts on empty needle.

Row 1: K1, [p1, k1] to end.

Rep row 1 twice more.

Work 22 rows in st st beg with a k row.

Now work across all 34 sts.

Next row: K16, m1, k2, m1, k to end. *(36 sts)*

Work 11 rows in st st beg with a p row.

Next row: [K1, p1] to end.

Rep last row once more.

Bind (cast) off keeping to the k1, p1 patt.

TO MAKE UP PAJAMAS

For pajama jacket, sew sleeve seams. Insert sleeves into armholes of main piece and stitch in place from the inside. Sew buttons in place using a separated strand of C. The gaps between the knitted stitches can be used for buttonholes. For pants, sew inside leg and back seams. Weave in all loose ends.

little teddy

HEAD AND BODY

(MAKE 2)

Cast on 10 sts in D.

Work 8 rows in st st beg with a k row.

Row 9: [Ssk] twice, k2, [k2tog] twice. *(6 sts)*

Row 10: P2tog, p2, p2tog tbl. *(4 sts)*

Row 11: K1, [m1, k1] to end. *(7 sts)*

Row 12: Purl.

Row 13: K1, m1 below, k3, m1 below, k1. *(9 sts)*

Row 14: Purl.

Row 15: K1, m1 below, k5, m1 below, k1. *(11 sts)*

Work 5 rows in st st beg with a p row.

Bind (cast) off.

ARMS

(MAKE 2)

Cast on 5 sts in D.

Work 6 rows in st st beg with a k row.

Break yarn, thread through sts, and secure.

LEGS

(MAKE 2)

Cast on 7 sts in D.

Work 4 rows in st st beg with a k row.

Row 5: K1, ssk, K1, k2tog, k1. *(5 sts)*

Break yarn, thread through rem sts, and secure.

EARS

(MAKE 2)

Using D3 (3.25mm) crochet hook make a length of 4 crochet chain stitches (see page 125) in D. Fasten off, leaving yarn tails both ends.

TO MAKE UP TEDDY

Sew two body and head pieces together, leaving lower edge open. Stuff and close lower edge.

Sew seams on arms and legs and stitch in place, using photograph as a guide. For eyes, separate a length of B into two thinner strands. Use this to work two French knots (see page 124) for the eyes. Use the same yarn to work a small coil of chain stitch (see page 124) for nose with a single vertical straight stitch underneath. Tie ribbon in bow around neck.

Nadia the Gymnast

Nadia loves to show her talents on the asymmetric bars and balance beam, never mind all those multiple flips and double pikes on the floor. Dressed in her new leotard with its contemporary squiggle design, she knows she'll look a million dollars on the medal podium as well as during the competition itself.

you will need

YARN AND MATERIALS

Debbie Bliss Baby Cashmerino (55% wool, 33% acrylic, 12% cashmere), 137yd (125m) per 1¾oz (50g) ball of sport weight (light DK) yarn
  ¾ ball Mink 64 (A)— head and body, arms, legs
  ¼ ball Black 300 (B)—hair and eyes
  ¼ ball Lipstick Pink 78 (C)—leotard
  Small amount of Candy Pink 06 (D)—leotard
  ¼ ball Kingfisher 72 (E)—leotard
  Very small amount of Mint 03 (F)—eyeshadow

Very small amount of coral, red, or pink embroidery floss (thread) or yarn—mouth

⅜in (10mm) gray button
2 x ¼in (6mm) gold beads
1oz (30g) polyester toy filling

NEEDLES AND EQUIPMENT

US3 (3.25mm) knitting needles

Yarn sewing needle

Large-eyed embroidery needle

Pins

Water-soluble marker

Coloring pencil in deep pink or red

GAUGE (TENSION)

Approximately 25 stitches and 34 rows to 4in (10cm) over st st (see also page 114)

ABBREVIATIONS

See page 127

main doll

Work as for basic pattern on page 9. Work head and body pieces, arms and legs in A.

HAIR
(MAKE 1)
Cast on 18 sts in B.
Work 4 rows in st st beg with a k row.
Row 5: Ssk, k to last 2 sts, k2tog. *(16 sts)*
Row 6: Purl.
Rep last 2 rows twice more. *(12 sts)*

Row 11: Inc, k to last 2 sts, inc, k1. *(14 sts)*
Row 12: Purl.
Row 13: Inc, k4, bind (cast) off 6 sts, (1 st rem on needle from binding/casting off), k2, inc, k1. *(2 groups of 6 sts)*
Work on last group of 6 sts only, leaving rem sts on needle.

Next row: Purl.
Next row: Ssk, k2, inc, k1.
Next row: P to last 2 sts, p2tog tbl.
(5 sts)
Next row: Ssk, k to end. *(4 sts)*
Next row: P2tog, p2tog tbl. *(2 sts)*
Next row: K2tog. *(1 st)*
Fasten off.
Rejoin yarn to rem sts on WS of work.
Next row: Purl.
Next row: Inc, k to last 2 sts, k2tog.
Next row: P2tog, p to end. *(5 sts)*
Next row: K to last 2 sts, k2tog.
(4 sts)
Next row: P2tog, p2tog tbl. *(2 sts)*
Next row: K2tog. *(1 st)*
Fasten off.

BUN
Cast on 3 sts in B.
Row 1: [Inc] 3 times. *(6 sts)*
Row 2: Purl.
Row 3: [Inc] 6 times. *(12 sts)*
Row 4: Purl.
Row 5: [K2tog] 6 times. *(6 sts)*
Row 6: [P2tog] 3 times. *(3 sts)*
Break yarn and thread through
rem sts.

TO MAKE UP DOLL
Make up main doll as explained on
page 9.
For eyes, work French knots (see page
124) using B. For the eyeshadow,
work a short, curved row of chain
stitch (see page 124) just above the
eye, using F. Embroider mouth in
straight stitch (see page 124) using
embroidery floss (thread) or a
separated strand of yarn. Work nose
by working a couple of chain stitches
in A, in a short vertical line. To make
the nose slightly more prominent, work
another couple of chain stitches over
the ones you have just sewn. For the
ears, work a few chain stitches in A, in

a short vertical line at the side of the
head, in line with the eyes. Then work
another row of chain stitches on top to
make the ears a bit more prominent.
Stitch beads in place for earrings,
using the photograph as a guide. Add
a bit of color to the cheeks using the
coloring pencil. Seam the hair piece to
form a cap shape. Pin then oversew
(see page 125) the hair piece to head,
using matching yarn. For bun, run yarn
tail around the outside of the knitted
piece, very close to the edge. Pull up
into a small sphere shape, stuffing with
a small piece of filling as you go. Stitch
in place on top of the head. Weave in
all loose ends.

leotard

(MAKE 1)
Cast on 16 sts in C.
Knit 2 rows.
Break yarn and cast on another 16 sts
on the same needle.
Knit 2 rows but do not break yarn.
Now knit across all 32 sts.
Work 18 rows in st st beg with a
k row.
Break C and join in D.
Next row: Knit.
Break D and join in E.
Next row: Purl.
Next row: Knit.
Next row: K2, p to last 2 sts, k2.
Next row: K6, k2tog, turn and work
on 7 sts just worked, leaving rem sts
on needle.
Next row: P to last 2 sts, k2.
Next row: K5, k2tog. *(6 sts)*
Next row: P to last 2 sts, k2.
Break yarn and rejoin it to rem 24 sts
on RS of work.
Next row: Ssk, k12, k2tog, turn and
work on 14 sts just worked, leaving
rem sts on needle.
Next row: Purl.
Next row: Ssk, k10, k2tog. *(12 sts)*
Next row: Purl.
Break yarn and rejoin it to rem sts on
RS of work.
Next row: Ssk, k to end. *(7 sts)*
Next row: K2, p to end.
Rep last 2 rows once more. *(6 sts)*
Now work across all 24 sts.
Knit 2 rows.
Bind (cast) off.

SLEEVES

(MAKE 2)
Cast on 12 sts in E.
Row 1: Knit.
Work 22 rows in st st beg with a
k row.
Bind (cast) off.

TO MAKE UP LEOTARD

Sew the crotch seam and the back
seam, up to D stripe. Insert sleeves
into armholes and stitch in place from
the inside. Using a yarn tail at the top
of the back of the leotard, use the
crochet hook to work a few crochet
chains (see page 125). Secure the free
end of the chain to form a button loop.
Sew button to corresponding side.
Using water-soluble pen, draw a loopy
squiggle around the lower part of the
leotard. Using D, embroider the
squiggle in chain stitch (see page 124),
remembering not to pull too tightly as
this will pull the leotard out of shape.
Weave in all loose ends.

Vintage Rosie

*Rosie loves a vintage look and often sews and knits her own
clothes using old patterns and retro fabrics and yarns.
She has two cats, Vincent and Dustin, whom she loves very much.*

you will need

YARN AND MATERIALS

FOR DOLL

Debbie Bliss Baby Cashmerino (55%
wool, 33% acrylic, 12% cashmere),
137yd (125m) per 1¾oz (50g) ball of
sport weight (light DK) yarn
- ½ ball of Camel 102 (A)—head and
  body, arms
- ¼ ball of Baby Pink 601 (B)—legs
- ¼ ball of Chocolate 11 (C)—hair
- ½ ball of Light Blue 202 (D)—dress
- Small amount of Citrus 18 (E)—
  dress trimming
- Small amount of Black 300
  (F)—eyes and shoes
- ¼ ball of Acid Yellow 91
  (G)—basket
- Very small amount of Flame 306
  (H)—flower on basket

Very small amount of coral, red, or
pink embroidery floss (thread) or
yarn—mouth

3 x ¼in (5mm) white buttons
for dress

1oz (30g) polyester toy filling

FOR CAT

Debbie Bliss Baby Cashmerino (55%
wool, 33% acrylic, 12% cashmere),
137yd (125m) per 1¾oz (50g) ball of
sport weight (light DK) yarn
- Small amount of Orange 92
  (marmalade cat) or Silver 12 (gray
  cat) (J)
- Small amount of White 100
  (marmalade cat) or Silver 12 (gray
  cat) (L)
- Very small amount of Black 300
  for features

Short length of ¼in (5mm) ribbon
for neck (optional)

Small amount of polyester toy filling

NEEDLES AND EQUIPMENT

US3 (3.25mm) knitting needles

D3 (3.25mm) crochet hook (or one of
similar size)

Yarn sewing needle

Large-eyed embroidery needle

Coloring pencil in deep pink or red

GAUGE (TENSION)

Approximately 25 stitches and
34 rows to 4in (10cm) over st st
(see also page 114)

ABBREVIATIONS

See page 127

main doll

Work as for basic pattern on page 9.
Work head and body piece and arms
in A.
Work legs in B.

HAIR MAIN PIECE
(MAKE 1)
Cast on 18 sts in C.
Work 4 rows in st st beg with a k row.
Row 5: Ssk, k to last 2 sts, k2tog.
(16 sts)
Row 6: Purl.
Rep last 2 rows twice more. *(12 sts)*
Row 11: Inc, k7, turn. *(9 sts)*
Next row: P2tog, p to end, turn.
(8 sts)
Next row: Inc, k5, k2tog, turn.
Next row: P2tog, p to end, turn.
(7 sts)
Next row: Inc, k4, k2tog, turn.
Next row: P2tog, p to end, turn.
(6 sts)
Next row: K4, k2tog, turn. *(5 sts)*
Next row: P2tog, p to end, turn.
(4 sts)
Next row: K2, k2tog, turn. *(3 sts)*
Next row: P2tog, p1. *(2 sts)*
Next row: K2tog. *(1 st)*
Fasten off.
Rejoin yarn to rem 4 sts on RS of work.
Next row: K to last st, inc. *(5 sts)*
Next row: Purl.
Rep last 2 rows once more. *(6 sts)*
Next row: Ssk, k to last st, inc.
Next row: Purl.
Next row: Ssk, k to end. *(5 sts)*
Next row: P to last 2 sts, p2tog.
(4 sts)
Rep last 2 rows once more. *(2 sts)*
Next row: K2tog. *(1 st)*
Fasten off.

BUNCHES

(MAKE 2)

Cast on 3 sts in C.

Row 1: [Inc] 3 times. *(6 sts)*

Row 2: Purl.

Row 3: [Inc] 6 times. *(12 sts)*

Row 4: Purl.

Row 5: [K2tog] 6 times. *(6 sts)*

Row 6: [P2tog] 3 times. *(3 sts)*

Break yarn and thread through
rem sts.

TO MAKE UP DOLL

Make up main doll as explained on
page 9. For eyes, work French knots
(see page 124) using F. Embroider
mouth by working two straight stitches
(see page 124) in embroidery floss
(thread). Work nose by working a
couple of chain stitches (see page
124) in A, in a short vertical line. To
make the nose slightly more
prominent, work another couple of
chain stitches over the ones you have
just sewn. Add a bit of color to the
cheeks using the coloring pencil.
Seam the hair piece to form a cap
shape. Pin then oversew (see page
125) the hair piece to head, using
matching yarn. For bunches, run yarn
tail around the outside of the knitted
pieces, very close to the edge. Pull up
into the teardrop shape, stuffing with a
tiny piece of stuffing as you go. Stitch
in place either side of the head.
Weave in all loose ends.

dress

(MAKE 1)

The dress is knitted from the
top down.

Cast on 24 sts in D.

Row 1: K6, m1, k1, m1, k10, m1, k1,
m1, k to end. *(28 sts)*

(When you are picking up a running
bar to make a stitch on the first row of
your knitting, it feels a little different—
don't worry about this; it will be ok.)

Row 2: K2, p to last 2 sts, k2.

Row 3: K6, m1, k3, m1, k10, m1, k3,
m1, k to end. *(32 sts)*

Row 4: K2, p to last 2 sts, k2.

Row 5: K6, m1, k5, m1, k10, m1, k5,
m1, k to end. *(36 sts)*

Row 6: K2, p to last 2 sts, k2.

Row 7: K6, m1, k7, m1, k10, m1, k7,
m1, k to end. *(40 sts)*

Row 8: K2, p5, bind (cast) off 7 sts
kwise, (1 st rem on needle from
binding/casting off) p11, bind (cast) off
7 sts kwise, (1 st rem on needle from
binding/casting off) p4, k2. *(26 sts)*

Row 9: K7, turn, cast on 3 sts, turn,
k12, turn, cast on 3 sts, turn, k to end.
(32 sts)

Row 10: K2, p to last 2 sts, k2.

Leave D at side of work and join in E.

Knit 2 rows.

Break E and cont in D.

Row 13: Knit.

Row 14: Purl.

Row 15: K8, m1, k1, m1, k14, m1,
k1, m1, k to end. *(36 sts)*

Work 3 rows in st st beg with a p row.

Row 19: K9, m1, k1, m1, k16, m1,
k1, m1, k to end. *(40 sts)*

Work 3 rows in st st beg with a p row.

Row 23: K10, m1, k1, m1, k18, m1,
k1, m1, k to end. *(44 sts)*

Work 3 rows in st st beg with a p row.

Row 27: K11, m1, k1, m1, k20, m1,
k1, m1, k to end. *(48 sts)*

Work 3 rows in st st beg with a p row.

Row 31: K12, m1, k1, m1, k22, m1,
k1, m1, k to end. *(52 sts)*

Work 3 rows in st st beg with a p row.

Row 35: K13, m1, k1, m1, k24, m1,
k1, m1, k to end. *(56 sts)*

Work 3 rows in st st beg with a p row.

Leave D at side and join in E.

Knit 4 rows.

Break E and cont in D.

Work 4 rows in st st beg with a k row.

Row 47: Purl.

Bind (cast) off pwise.

COLLAR

(MAKE 1)

With WS facing and E, pick up and
knit 24 sts along cast-on edge.

Row 2: K12, turn.

Knit 3 rows on these 12 sts only,
leaving rem sts on needle.

Bind (cast) off.

Rejoin yarn to rem sts on RS of work.

Knit 4 rows.

Bind (cast) off.

TO MAKE UP DRESS

Close the back seam of the dress, up
to the base of the back opening, using
mattress stitch (see page 125). Using
a yarn tail at the top of the back of the
dress, work a short crochet chain (see
page 125) using the crochet hook.
Secure the free end to form a button
loop. Sew button to corresponding
side. Sew remaining two buttons to
front of dress using the photograph as
a guide. Weave in all loose ends.

shoes

(MAKE 2)

Cast on 24 sts in F.

Work 4 rows in st st beg with a k row.

Row 5: K6, [ssk] 3 times, [k2tog]
3 times, k to end. *(18 sts)*

Bind (cast) off pwise.

TO MAKE UP SHOES

Fold shoe piece in half so that the right
side is on the inside and oversew sole
(see page 125). Turn the piece the
right way out and sew the back seam
using mattress stitch (see page 125).
Weave in all loose ends.

basket

(MAKE 2)
Cast on 8 sts in G leaving a 12in (30cm) on one of the pieces.
Row 1: [Inc] 8 times. *(16 sts)*
Row 2: Knit.
Row 3: K1, [p2, k1] to end.
Row 4: P1, [k2, p1] to end.
Row 5: Knit.
Row 6: Purl.
Rep rows 3–6 twice more.
Rep rows 3–4 once more.
Row 17: [Ssk] twice, k to last 4 sts, [k2tog] twice. *(12 sts)*
Bind (cast) off pwise.

TO MAKE UP BASKET
Sew side and lower seams using mattress stitch (see page 125). Use the long yarn tail at the top to crochet a 2in (5cm) chain (see page 125). Join the free end of the crochet chain to the opposite end of the basket to form the handle. Using H, embroider a daisy (see page 124). Weave in all loose ends.

cat

FACE
(MAKE 2)
Cast on 6 sts in J.
Row 1: Inc, k3, inc, k1. *(8 sts)*
Row 2: Purl.
Row 3: K1, m1, k to last st, m1, k1. *(10 sts)*
Row 4: Purl.
Rep rows 3–4 once more. *(12 sts)*
Work 4 rows in st st beg with a k row.
Row 11: K5, bind (cast) off 2 sts, k to end.

Work on last group of 5 sts only, leaving rem sts on needle.
Next row: P3, p2tog. *(4 sts)*
Next row: K2tog, k2. *(3 sts)*
Next row: Sl1 pwise, p2tog, psso. *(1 st)*
Fasten off.
Rejoin yarn to rem sts on WS of work.
Next row: P2tog, p to end. *(4 sts)*
Next row: K2, ssk. *(3 sts)*
Next row: Sl1 pwise, p2tog, psso. *(1 st)*
Fasten off.

BODY
(MAKE 1)
Cast on 5 sts in J.
Work 4 rows in st st.
Row 5: K1, m1, k to end. *(6 sts)*
Row 6: Purl.
Break yarn and leave sts on needle.
Cast on another 5 sts on needle with sts.
Work 4 rows in st st.
Row 5: K4, m1, k1. *(6 sts)*
Row 6: Purl.
Now work across all 12 sts.
Next row: K6, turn and cast on 4 sts, turn back and k rem sts.* *(16 sts)*
Work 17 rows in st st beg with a p row.
**Next row: K4, k2tog, bind (cast) off 4 sts, ssk using st rem from binding (casting) off as first slipped stitch, k to end. *(14 sts)*
Work on last group of 5 sts only, leaving rem sts on needle.
Work 4 rows in st st beg with a k row.
Bind (cast) off.
Rejoin yarn to rem 5 sts on WS of work.
Work 4 rows in st st beg with a k row.
Bind (cast) off.

BODY GUSSET
(MAKE 1)
Using L, work as for body from beg to *.
Next row: Purl.
Next row: Cast on 3 sts, k to end. *(19 sts)*
Next row: Cast on 3 sts, p to end. *(22 sts)*
Next row: Bind (cast) off 3 sts, k to end. *(19 sts)*
Next row: Bind (cast) off 3 sts, p to end. *(16 sts)*
Work as for body from ** to end.

TO MAKE UP CAT
Place two head pieces together and oversew (see page 125) around outside, leaving the lower edge open for turning and stuffing. Turn, stuff lightly then close gap. Place the body and gusset pieces right sides together and pin. The "peaks" on the gusset should reach up the main body piece to give the cat its shape under tail and chin. Oversew around the pieces, leaving a gap along one edge to turn and stuff. Turn, stuff lightly then close the gap. Using a divided length of black yarn work two French knots (see page 124) for the eyes then work a standard French knot for the nose and add a vertical straight stitch (see page 124) below it. Work straight stitches for the whiskers using a single split length of black yarn. Weave in all loose ends. Tie ribbon in a bow around cat's neck.

Hipster Henry

Henry knows that if you want to be a trendsetter and want to look cool, it's essential not to try too hard. A plain T-shirt, your favorite jeans, and a simple blazer will get your look started, but never forget the importance of a bag, a fancy pair of shoes, and the right kind of hat.

main doll

Work as for basic pattern on page 9. Work head and body pieces, arms and legs in A.

HAIR
(MAKE 1)
Cast on 19 sts in B.
Row 1: K1, [p1, k1] to end.
Rep row 1, 3 times more.
Row 5: P2tog, [k1, p1] to last 3 sts, k1, p2tog tbl. (17 sts)
Row 6: P1, [k1, p1] to end.
Row 7: Ssk, [p1, k1] to last 3 sts, p1, k2tog. (15 sts)
Row 8: K1, [p1, k1] to end.
Rep rows 5–6 once more. (13 sts)
Row 11: Inc pwise, [k1, p1] to last 2 sts, k1, inc pwise. (15 sts)
Row 12: K1, [p1, k1] to end.
Row 13: Inc, [p1, k1] to last 2 sts, p1, inc. (17 sts)
Row 14: P1, [k1, p1] to end.
Row 15: Inc pwise, [k1, p1] twice, bind (cast) off 7 sts, keeping to the k1, p1 patt, (1 st rem on needle from binding/casting off), k1, p1, k1, inc pwise. (12 sts)
Work on last group of 6 sts only, leaving rem sts on needle.
Next row: [K1, p1] twice, ssk. (5 sts)
Next row: P2tog, k1, p1, k1. (4 sts)
Next row: K1, p1, k2tog. (3 sts)
Next row: P2tog, k1. (2 sts)

Next row: K2tog. (1 st)
Fasten off.
Rejoin yarn to rem sts on WS of work.
Next row: K2tog, [p1, k1] twice. (5 sts)
Next row: K1, p1, k1, p2tog. (4 sts)
Next row: K2tog, p1, k1. (3 sts)
Next row: K1, p2tog. (2 sts)
Next row: K2tog. (1 st)
Fasten off.

TO MAKE UP DOLL
Make up main doll as explained on page 9. For eyes, work French knots (see page 124) using B. Embroider mouth in straight stitch (see page 124) using embroidery floss (thread) or a separated strand of yarn. Work nose by working a couple of chain stitches (see page 124) in A, in a short vertical line. To make the nose slightly more prominent, work another couple of chain stitches over the ones you have just sewn. For the ears, work a few chain stitches in A, in a short vertical line at the side of the head, in line with the eyes. Then work another row of chain stitches on top to make the ears a bit more prominent. Add a bit of color to the cheeks using the coloring pencil.
Seam the hair piece to form a cap shape. Pin then oversew (see page 125) the hair piece to head, using matching yarn.
Weave in all loose ends.

you will need

YARN AND MATERIALS
Debbie Bliss Baby Cashmerino (55% wool, 33% acrylic, 12% cashmere), 137yd (125m) per 1¾oz (50g) ball of sport weight (light DK) yarn
  ½ ball of Teddy 308 (A)—head and body, arms, legs
  ¼ ball of Black 300 (B)—hair, eyes, laces, soles of shoes
  ½ ball of Sea Green 99 (C)—jacket
  ¼ ball of White 100 (D)—T-shirt and shoe uppers
  ¼ ball of Pool 71 (E)—jeans
  ¼ ball of Baby Blue 204 (F)—peaked hat
  Small amount of Primrose 01 (G)—bag
Very small amount of coral, red, or pink embroidery floss (thread) or yarn—mouth
2 x ⁵⁄₁₆in (8mm) black buttons
⁵⁄₁₆in (8mm) white button
1oz (30g) polyester toy filling

NEEDLES AND EQUIPMENT
US3 (3.25mm) knitting needles
D3 (3.25mm) crochet hook (or one of similar size)
Yarn sewing needle
Large-eyed embroidery needle
Pins
Coloring pencil in deep pink or red

GAUGE (TENSION)
Approximately 25 stitches and 34 rows to 4in (10cm) over st st (see also page 114)

ABBREVIATIONS
See page 127

jacket

BACK AND FRONT

(MAKE 1)

Cast on 42 sts in C.

Row 1: Inc, k to end. *(43 sts)*
Row 2: Inc, k to end. *(44 sts)*
Row 3: K2, p to last 2 sts, k2.
Row 4: Knit.
Row 5: K2, p to last 2 sts, k2.
Rep rows 4–5, 7 times more.
Row 20: K11, turn.
Work on these 11 sts only, leaving rem sts on needle.
Next row: P to last 2 sts, k2.
Next row: Knit.
Next row: P to last 2 sts, k2.
Rep last 2 rows twice more.
Next row: Knit.
Break yarn and rejoin it to rem 11 sts on RS of work.
Next row: K22, turn.
Work on these 22 sts only, leaving rem sts on needle.
Work 8 rows in st st beg with a p row.
Break yarn and rejoin it to rem sts on RS of work.
Next row: Knit.
Next row: K2, p to end.
Rep last 2 rows 3 times more.
Next row: Knit.
Now work across all 44 sts.
Next row: K2, p to last 2 sts, k2.
Next row: Bind (cast) off 2 sts pwise, k6, ssk, k2tog, k2, ssk, k10, k2tog, k2, ssk, k2tog, k to end. *(36 sts)*
Next row: Bind (cast) off 2 sts, p to last 2 sts, k2. *(34 sts)*
Next row: K4, [ssk] twice, [k2tog] 3 times, k6, [ssk] 3 times, [k2tog] twice, k to end. *(24 sts)*
Knit 4 rows.
Bind (cast) off.

SLEEVES

(MAKE 2)

Cast on 16 sts in C.

Row 1: Knit.
Work 18 rows in st st beg with a k row.
Bind (cast) off.

POCKET

(MAKE 1)

Cast on 5 sts in C.

Row 1: Knit.
Work 4 rows in st st beg with a k row.
Bind (cast) off pwise.

TO MAKE UP JACKET

Sew sleeve seams. Insert into armholes and stitch in place from the inside. Sew black buttons onto jacket using separated strand of B. The gaps between the knitted stitches can be used for buttonholes. Sew pocket in place on right front. Weave in all loose ends.

t-shirt

The T-shirt is knitted from the top down.

(MAKE 1)

Cast on 24 sts in D.

Row 1: Knit.
Row 2: K6, m1, k1, m1, k10, m1, k1, m1, k to end. *(28 sts)*
Row 3: K2, p to last 2 sts, k2.
Row 4: K6, m1, k3, m1, k10, m1, k3, m1, k to end. *(32 sts)*
Row 5: K2, p to last 2 sts, k2.
Row 6: K6, m1, k5, m1, k10, m1, k5, m1, k to end. *(36 sts)*
Row 7: K2, p to last 2 sts, k2.
Row 8: K6, m1, k7, m1, k10, m1, k7, m1, k to end. *(40 sts)*
Row 9: K2, p5, bind (cast) off 7 sts kwise, (1 st rem on needle from binding/casting off), p11, bind (cast) off 7 sts kwise, (1 st rem on needle from binding/casting off), p4, k2. *(26 sts)*
Row 10: K7, turn, cast on 3 sts, turn, k12, turn, cast on 3 sts, turn, k to end. *(32 sts)*
Row 11: K2, p to last 2 sts, k2.
Work 14 rows in st st beg with a k row.
Row 26: Purl.
Bind (cast) off.

TO MAKE UP T-SHIRT

Sew the back seam of the T-shirt, from the lower edge up to the base of the back opening worked in garter stitch. Using a yarn tail at the top of the back of the T-shirt, use the crochet hook to work a few crochet chains (see page 125). Secure the free end of the chain to form a button loop. Sew white button to corresponding side. Weave in all loose ends.

jeans

(MAKE 1)

Cast on 18 sts in E.

Row 1: Knit.
Work 26 rows in st st beg with a k row.
Break yarn and leave sts on needle.
Cast on 18 sts on empty needle.
Row 1: Knit.
Work 26 rows in st st beg with a k row but do not break yarn.
Now work across all 36 sts.
Work 11 rows in st st beg with a k row.
Next row: [K1, p1] to end.
Rep last row once more.
Bind (cast) off keeping to the k1, p1 patt.

TO MAKE UP JEANS

Sew inside leg and back seams. Weave in all loose ends.

peaked hat

BRIM
(MAKE 1)
Cast on 36 sts in F.
Knit 2 rows.
Row 3: P3, [inc pwise, p2] to end.
(47 sts)
Work 6 rows in st st beg with a k row.
Bind (cast) off.

CROWN
(MAKE 1)
Cast on 9 sts in F.
Row 1: Inc, k to last 2 sts, inc, k1.
(11 sts)
Row 2: Purl.
Rep rows 1–2, 3 times more. *(17 sts)*
Work 2 rows in st st beg with a k row.
Row 11: Ssk, k to last 2 sts, k2tog.
(15 sts)
Row 12: Purl.
Rep rows 11–12 twice more. *(11 sts)*
Row 17: Ssk, k to last 2 sts, k2tog.
(9 sts)
Bind (cast) off pwise.

TO MAKE UP AND WORK PEAK
Make up the main part of hat before
working the peak. Sew the short sides
of the brim to form a circle. Attach the
crown of the hat to the brim from the
inside, with seam at the center back.

PEAK
Using F, with RS facing, pick up and
knit 14 sts across the center front of
the brim.
Row 1: Purl.
Row 2: K1, ssk, k to last 3 sts, k2tog,
k1. *(12 sts)*
Row 3: P2tog, p to last 2 sts, p2tog
tbl. *(10 sts)*
Rep rows 2–3 once more. *(6 sts)*
Row 6: K1, m1, k to last st, m1, k1.
(8 sts)
Row 7: P1, m1 pwise, p to last st, m1
pwise, p1. *(10 sts)*
Rep rows 6–7 once more. *(14 sts)*
Bind (cast) off.
Fold the peak in half to the inside of
the hat and oversew (see page 125)
the sides and the bound- (cast)- off
edge under the brim.

messenger bag

BAG
(MAKE 1)
Cast on 13 sts in G.
Row 1: K1, [p1, k1] to end.
Rep last row 41 times.
Bind (cast) off keeping to the k1,
p1 pattern.

STRAP
(MAKE 1)
Cast on 48 sts in G.
Row 1: Knit.
Bind (cast) off.

TO MAKE UP BAG
Fold bottom edge up to form bag,
leaving top third free to form flap.
Stitch side seams. Sew strap to sides
of bag. Weave in all loose ends.

shoes

(MAKE 2)
Cast on 24 sts in B.
Knit 2 rows
Break B and join in D.
Work 4 rows in st st beg with a k row.
Row 7: K6, [ssk] 3 times, [k2tog]
3 times, k to end. *(18 sts)*
Row 8: Purl.
Row 9: K5, [ssk] twice, [k2tog] twice,
k to end. *(14 sts)*
Row 10: Knit.
Bind (cast) off.

TO MAKE UP SHOES
Fold shoe pieces in half so that the
right side is on the inside and oversew
(see page 125) sole. Turn the pieces
the right way out and sew the back
seams. Using B, work two straight
stitches (see page 124) on front of
shoes to represent laces. Weave in all
loose ends.

Renée the Rabbit

She's fast and skittish and loves scampering through fields and meadows and munching on grass and clover. But when she's not doing that, Renée loves sitting in her burrow, chattering away to all her brothers and sisters and working out how to keep away from foxes.

you will need

YARN AND MATERIALS

Debbie Bliss Baby Cashmerino (55% wool, 33% acrylic, 12% cashmere), 137yd (125m) per 1¾oz (50g) ball of sport weight (light DK) yarn
  ¾ ball of Slate 09 (A)—main rabbit
  ½ ball of Candy Pink 06 (B)—tunic
  ¼ ball of Mint 03 (C)—Capri pants
  Very small amounts of Black 300 and White 100—eyes, mouth

A small fabric flower

1oz (30g) polyester toy filling

NEEDLES AND EQUIPMENT

US3 (3.25mm) knitting needles

Yarn sewing needle

Large-eyed embroidery needle

GAUGE (TENSION)

Approximately 25 stitches and 34 rows to 4in (10cm) over st st (see also page 114)

ABBREVIATIONS

m1 below = Find the top loop of the stitch below the next stitch on the left-hand needle. Insert the tip of the right-hand needle into that top loop from front to back. If this is difficult try picking up the stitch from the back, hold it with the left thumb and forefinger, then remove the needle and reinsert it into the loop from front to back. Knit into the stitch then knit into the stitch on the needle (see page 121).

See also page 127

body and head

FRONT

(MAKE 1)
Cast on 18 sts in A.
Work 28 rows in st st beg with a k row.

Row 29: [Ssk] 4 times, k2, [k2tog] 4 times. *(10 sts)*
Work 3 rows in st st beg with a k row.
Row 33: K1, m1 below, k to last 2 sts, m1 below, k1. *(12 sts)*
Row 34: Purl.
Rep rows 33–34 twice more.* *(16 sts)*

Row 39: K1, m1 below, k6, m1, k6, m1 below, k1. *(19 sts)*
Row 40 and every WS row: Purl.
Row 41: K1, ssk, k6, m1, k1, m1, k6, k2tog, k1.
Row 43: K1, ssk, k5, m1, k3, m1, k5, k2tog, k1.

Row 45: K1, ssk, k4, m1, k5, m1, k4, k2tog, k1.
Row 47: K1, ssk, k3, m1, k7, m1, k3, k2tog, k1.
Row 49: K1, ssk, k2, m1, k9, m1, k2, k2tog, k1.
Row 51: K1, ssk, k to last 3 sts, k2tog, k1. *(17 sts)*
Row 52: Purl.
Rep rows 51–52 once more. *(15 sts)*
Row 55: K2, ssk, k to last 3 sts, k2tog, k1. *(13 sts)*
Bind (cast) off pwise.

BACK
(MAKE 1)
Work as for front to *.
Row 39: K1, m1 below, k to last 2 sts, m1 below, k1. *(18 sts)*
Work 11 rows in st st beg with a p row.
Row 51: K1, ssk, k to last 3 sts, k2tog, k1. *(16 sts)*
Row 52: Purl.
Rep rows 51–52 once more. *(14 sts)*
Row 55: K2, ssk, k to last 3 sts, k2tog, k1. *(12 sts)*
Bind (cast) off pwise.

ARMS
(MAKE 2)
Cast on 11 sts in A.
Work 32 rows in st st beg with a k row.
Row 33: K1, ssk, k5, k2tog, k1. *(9 sts)*
Break yarn and thread it through rem sts.

LEGS
(MAKE 2)
Cast on 30 sts in A.
Work 4 rows in st st beg with a k row.
Row 5: K9, [ssk] 3 times, [k2tog] 3 times, k to end. *(24 sts)*
Row 6: Purl.
Row 7: K6, [ssk] 3 times, [k2tog] 3 times, k to end. *(18 sts)*
Row 8: Purl.
Row 9: K5, [ssk] twice, [k2tog] twice, k to end. *(14 sts)*
Row 10: Purl.
Row 11: K5, ssk, k2tog, k to end. *(12 sts)*
Work 27 rows in st st beg with a p row.
Bind (cast) off.

EARS
(MAKE 2)
Cast on 10 sts in A.
Work 6 rows in st st beg with a k row.
Row 7: K2, ssk, k2, k2tog, k2. *(8 sts)*
Row 8: Purl.
Row 9: K1, ssk, k2, k2tog, k1. *(6 sts)*
Row 10: Purl.
Row 11: K1, ssk, k2tog, k1. *(4 sts)*
Row 12: Purl.
Row 13: Ssk, k2tog. *(2 sts)*
Row 14: P2tog. *(1 st)*
Fasten off.

TO MAKE UP DOLL
Make up main animal in the same way as the basic doll explained on page 9. For the ears, fold the piece in half lengthwise and join seam. Sew in position using the photograph as a guide, keeping seam at center back of ear. For eyes, work French knots (see page 124) using black yarn. Using white yarn, work a circle of chain stitch (see page 124) around each French knot. Using black yarn, work three stitches in a Y shape for nose, using the photograph as a guide. Weave in all loose ends.

tunic

(MAKE 1)
Cast on 48 sts in B.
Row 1: [K2, p1] to end.
Row 2: [K1, yo, k2, pass yo st over 2 k sts] to end.
Rep last 2 rows twice more.
Work 12 rows in st st beg with a k row.
Row 19: K9, ssk, k2, k2tog, k18, ssk, k2, k2tog, k to end. *(44 sts)*
Work 3 rows in st st beg with a p row.
Row 23: K8, ssk, k2, k2tog, k16, ssk, k2, k2tog, k to end. *(40 sts)*
Work 3 rows in st st beg with a p row.
Row 27: K7, ssk, k2, k2tog, k14, ssk, k2, k2tog, k to end. *(36 sts)*
Work 3 rows in st st beg with a p row.
Row 31: Bind (cast) off 9 sts, (1 st rem on needle from binding/casting off), k17, bind (cast) off rem sts. *(18 sts)*
Rejoin yarn to WS of work.
Next row: P2tog, p to last 2 sts, p2tog tbl. *(16 sts)*
Next row: K2, ssk, k to last 4 sts, k2tog, k2. *(14 sts)*
Next row: K2, p to last 2 sts, k2.
Rep last 2 rows once more. *(12 sts)*
Knit 2 rows.
Next row: K3, bind (cast) off 6 sts pwise, k to end.
Knit 12 rows on each group of 3 sts.
Bind (cast) off.

TO MAKE UP TUNIC
Sew back seam of tunic. Sew short ends of strap to corresponding positions on back of tunic. Sew fabric flower in place. Weave in all loose ends.

capri pants

(MAKE 1)
Cast on 18 sts in C.
Row 1: Knit.
Row 2: K1, [yo, k2tog] to last st, k1.
Row 3: Knit.
Work 18 rows in st st beg with a k row.
Break yarn and leave sts on needle.
Cast on 18 sts on empty needle.
Row 1: Knit.
Row 2: K1, [yo, k2tog] to last st, k1.
Row 3: Knit.
Work 18 rows in st st beg with a k row but do not break yarn.
Now work across all 36 sts.
Work 14 rows in st st beg with a k row.
Next row: [K1, p1] to end.
Rep last row once more.
Bind (cast) off keeping to the k1, p1 patt.

TO MAKE UP PANTS
Sew inside leg and back seams.
Weave in all loose ends.

Superhero Stan

Stan believes that dressing up is not just for parties. It's also for going to the supermarket, going to tea at his best friend's house, and going to see his grandma. Stan loves dressing up as an astronaut, a police officer, and a magician, but there are no prizes for guessing his favorite outfit.

main doll

Work as for basic pattern on page 9. Work head and body pieces and arms in A. Work legs in B.

HAIR

(MAKE 1)
Cast on 18 sts in C.
Work 4 rows in st st beg with a k row.
Row 5: Ssk, k to last 2 sts, k2tog. *(16 sts)*
Row 6: Purl.
Rep last 2 rows twice more. *(12 sts)*
Row 11: Inc, k to last 2 sts, inc, k1. *(14 sts)*
Row 12: Purl.
Rep last 2 rows once more. *(16 sts)*
Row 15: Inc, k4, bind (cast) off 6 sts, (1 st rem on needle from binding/casting off), k2, inc, k1. *(2 groups of 6 sts)*
Work on 6 sts just worked only, leaving rem sts on needle.
Next row: Purl.
Next row: Ssk, k to end. *(5 sts)*
Next row: P to last 2 sts, p2tog tbl. *(4 sts)*
Next row: Ssk, k to end. *(3 sts)*
Next row: P1, p2tog tbl. *(2 sts)*
Next row: Ssk. *(1 st)*
Fasten off.
Rejoin yarn to rem sts on WS of work.

Next row: Purl.
Next row: K to last 2 sts, k2tog. *(5 sts)*
Next row: P2tog, p to end. *(4 sts)*
Next row: K2, k2tog. *(3 sts)*
Next row: P2tog, p1. *(2 sts)*
Next row: K2tog. *(1 st)*
Fasten off.

TO MAKE UP DOLL

Make up main doll as explained on page 9. For eyes, work French knots (see page 124) using F. Embroider mouth in straight stitch (see page 124) using embroidery floss (thread) or a separated strand of yarn. Work nose by working a couple of chain stitches (see page 124) in A, in a short vertical line. To make the nose slightly more prominent, work another couple of chain stitches over the ones you have just sewn. For the ears, work a few chain stitches in A, in a short vertical line at the side of the head, in line with the eyes. Then work another row of chain stitches on top to make the ears a bit more prominent. Add a bit of color to the cheeks using the coloring pencil. Seam the hair piece to form a cap shape. Pin then oversew (see page 125) the hair piece to head, using matching yarn. Embroider curl at front of hair in chain stitch using photograph as a guide.
Weave in all loose ends.

sweater

FRONT AND BACK

(MAKE 2)
Cast on 22 sts in B.
Row 1: Knit.
Work 8 rows in st st beg with a k row. Mark beg and end of last row with stitch markers or small safety pins. Also mark the middle two stitches of the row (the 11th and 12th sts) which will indicate where you will begin working the star motif on the front (see below).
Work 10 rows in st st beg with a k row.
Row 20: K2, ssk, k to last 4 sts, k2tog, k2. *(20 sts)*
Row 21: Purl.
Rep rows 20–21 once more. *(18 sts)*
Work 6 rows in st st beg with a k row.
Row 30: Bind (cast) off 3 sts, k to end. *(15 sts)*
Row 31: Bind (cast) off 3 sts pwise, p to end. *(12 sts)*
Work 3 rows in st st beg with a k row.
Bind (cast) off kwise loosely.

SLEEVES

Join neck edges and shoulders of front and back pieces. With RS facing, pick up and knit 8 sts from one stitch marker or safety pin to shoulder edges and another 8 sts from shoulder edges to second stitch marker or safety pin. *(16 sts)*
Work 19 rows in st st beg with a p row.
Knit 2 rows.
Bind (cast) off loosely. Rep for second sleeve.

TO MAKE UP SWEATER

Using Swiss embroidery technique (see page 125) work star in E following the chart below. Add an extra single chain stitch between the top two stitches to make the star extra pointy. Join side and sleeve seams. Weave in all loose ends.

- ■ Sapphire 89
- □ Acid Yellow 91

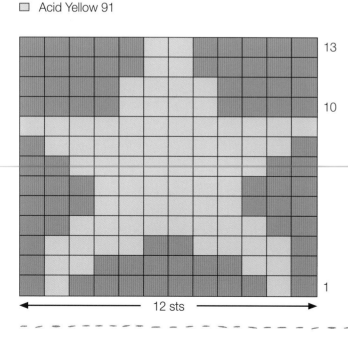

13

10

1

← 12 sts →

cape

(MAKE 1)

Cast on 30 sts in D.

Row 1: Purl.

Row 2: Knit.

Row 3: K2, p to last 2 sts, k2.

Rep rows 2–3, 19 times more.

Row 42: K6, [ssk] 3 times, k6, [k2tog] 3 times, k to end. *(24 sts)*

Row 43: Knit.

Bind (cast) off, leaving a long yarn tail.

TO MAKE UP CAPE

Using the crochet hook and yarn tail from binding (casting) off, work a 3½-in (9-cm) crochet chain (see page 125) for one side of the fastening. Make a matching crochet chain and sew it onto the other side to form the second fastening. Weave in all loose ends.

shorts

(MAKE 1)

Cast on 18 sts in D.

Work 13 rows in st st beg with a p row.

Break yarn and leave sts on needle.

Cast on 18 sts in D on needle without sts.

Work 13 rows in st st beg with a p row.

Now work across all 36 sts.

Work 12 rows in st st beg with a k row.

Next row: [K1, p1] to end.

Rep last row once more.

Bind (cast) off keeping to the k1, p1 patt.

TO MAKE UP SHORTS

Sew inside leg and back seams. Weave in all loose ends.

boots

(MAKE 2)

Cast on 26 sts in D.

Knit 3 rows.

Work 4 rows in st st beg with a k row.

Row 8: K7, [ssk] 3 times, [k2tog] 3 times, k to end. *(20 sts)*

Row 9: Purl.

Row 10: K6, [ssk] twice, [k2tog] twice, k to end. *(16 sts)*

Work 6 rows in st st beg with a p row.

Bind (cast) off kwise loosely.

TO MAKE UP BOOTS

Fold boot pieces in half so that the right side is on the inside and oversew (see page 125) sole. Turn the pieces the right way out and sew the back seams. Weave in all loose ends.

Beach Babe Jessica

Jessica loves the simple things in life, so long as they make her look good. Whether she's on vacation or just a day trip, when the sun peeks out from the clouds she's the first to stash a few essentials in her bag and head down to the beach. Splashing around and soaking up the rays, life couldn't be much better.

you will need

YARN AND MATERIALS

Debbie Bliss Baby Cashmerino (55% wool, 33% acrylic; 12% cashmere), 137yd (125m) per 1¾oz (50g) ball of sport weight (light DK) yarn
- ¾ ball of Clotted Cream 65 (A)—head and body, arms, legs
- ¼ ball of Drake 302 (B)—flip flop sandals, beach bag, hat bow
- ¼ ball of Acid Yellow 91 (C)—hair
- ¼ ball of Lipstick Pink 78 (D)—bikini, beach bag handles, sunglasses frames
- ¼ ball of Apple 02 (E)—bikini, hat
- ¼ ball of Rose Pink 94 (F)—towel
- Very small amount of Black 300 (G)—eyes

Very small amount of coral, red, or pink embroidery floss (thread) or yarn—mouth

2 small bright pink fabric flowers for shoes

1 larger bright pink fabric flower for bag

Small amount of blue acetate

PVA glue

Waxed paper

1oz (30g) polyester toy filling

NEEDLES AND EQUIPMENT

US3 (3.25mm) knitting needles

D3 (3.25mm) crochet hook (or one of similar size)

G6 (4.5mm) crochet hook (or one of similar size)

Yarn sewing needle

Large-eyed embroidery needle

Pins

Coloring pencil in deep pink or red

GAUGE (TENSION)

Approximately 25 stitches and 34 rows to 4in (10cm) over st st (see also page 114)

ABBREVIATIONS

See page 127

main doll

Work as for basic pattern on page 9. Work head and body pieces and arms in A.

LEGS

(MAKE 2)

Cast on 24 sts in B.

Knit 2 rows.

Break B and join in A.

Work 2 rows in st st beg with a k row.

Row 5: K6, [ssk] 3 times, [k2tog] 3 times, k to end. *(18 sts)*

Row 6: Purl.

Row 7: K5, [ssk] twice, [k2tog] twice, k to end. *(14 sts)*

Row 8: Purl.

Row 9: K5, ssk, k2tog, k to end. *(12 sts)*

Work 29 rows in st st beg with a p row.

Bind (cast) off.

HAIR

(MAKE 1)

Cast on 18 sts in C.

Work 8 rows in st st beg with a k row.

Row 9: Ssk, k to last 2 sts, k2tog. *(16 sts)*

Row 10: Purl.

Rep last 2 rows twice more. *(12 sts)*

Row 13: Inc, k7, turn. *(9 sts)*

Next row: P2tog, p to end, turn. *(8 sts)*

Next row: Inc, k5, k2tog, turn.

Next row: P2tog, p to end, turn. *(7 sts)*

Next row: Inc, k4, k2tog, turn.

Next row: P2tog, p to end, turn. *(6 sts)*

Next row: K4, k2tog, turn. *(5 sts)*

Next row: P2tog, p to end, turn. *(4 sts)*

Next row: K2, k2tog, turn. *(3 sts)*

Next row: P2tog, p1. *(2 sts)*

Next row: K2tog. *(1 st)*

Fasten off.

Rejoin yarn to rem 4 sts on RS of work.

Next row: K to last st, inc. *(5 sts)*

Next row: Purl.

Rep last 2 rows once more. *(6 sts)*

Next row: Ssk, k to last st, inc.

Next row: Purl.

Next row: Ssk, k to end. *(5 sts)*

Next row: P to last 2 sts, p2tog. *(4 sts)*

Rep last 2 rows once more. *(2 sts)*

Next row: K2tog. *(1 st)*

Fasten off.

Using G6 (4.5mm) crochet hook and C doubled, make two 8in (20cm) crochet chains (see page 125).

TO MAKE UP DOLL

Make up main doll as explained on page 9. For eyes, work French knots (see page 124) using G. Embroider mouth in straight stitch (see page 124) using embroidery floss (thread) or a separated strand of yarn. Work nose by working a couple of chain stitches (see page 124) in A, in a short vertical line. To make the nose slightly more prominent, work another couple of chain stitches over the ones you have just sewn. For belly button, work a stitch from the back to the front of the doll and pull slightly before securing. Add a bit of color to the cheeks using the coloring pencil.

Seam the hair piece to form a cap shape. Pin then oversew (see page 125) the hair piece to head, using matching yarn. Arrange each crochet chain into two loops and sew to side of head, using the photograph as a guide. Weave in all loose ends.

bikini

SHORTS

(MAKE 1)

Note: When slipping sts, slip pwise but with yarn at back of work.

Cast on 16 sts in D.

Row 1: Knit

Row 2: [K1, sl1] to end.

Row 3: Knit.

Leave D at side and join in E.

Row 4: [Sl1, k1] to end.

Row 5: Knit.

Leave E at side and use D.

Rep rows 2–3 once more.

Break yarns.

Cast on 16 sts in D on empty needle.

Rep rows 1–7 (rows on first needle) for second leg but do not break yarn.

Now work across all 32 sts.

Rep rows 4–5 in E.

Rep rows 2–3 in D.

Rep last 4 rows 3 times more.

Break E and work rem of shorts in D.

Next row: Knit.

Next row: [K1, p1] to end.

Rep last row once more.

Bind (cast) off keeping to the k1, p1 patt.

TOP

(MAKE 1)

Cast on 32 sts in D.

Row 1: Knit

Leave D at side and join in E.

Row 2: [K1, sl1] to end.

Row 3: Knit.

Leave E at side and join in D.

Row 4: [Sl1, k1] to end.

Row 5: Knit.

Rep rows 2–5 (last 4 rows) once more.

Break E and work rem of top in D.

Row 10: Knit.

Bind (cast) off.

STRAP

(MAKE 1)

Cast on 25 sts in D.

Bind (cast) off.

TO MAKE UP BIKINI

For bikini shorts, sew inside leg and back seams. For bikini top, sew back seam. Sew short edges of strap to front of top, then sew center of strap to back of bikini top to make two separate shoulder straps.

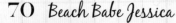

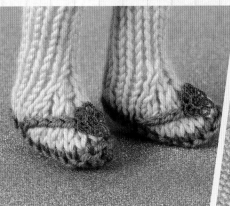

hat

(MAKE 1)
Cast on 36 sts in E.
Work 8 rows in st st beg with a k row.
Row 9: [K2tog] to end. *(18 sts)*
Row 10: Purl.
Row 11: [K2tog] to end. *(9 sts)*
Row 12: [P2tog] twice, p1, [p2tog] twice. *(5 sts)*
Break yarn, thread through rem sts, and secure.
With RS facing, pick up and knit 35 sts along cast-on edge for brim.
Next row: P1, [inc pwise, p1] to end. *(52 sts)*
Work 5 rows in st st beg with a k row.
Next row: Knit.
Bind (cast) off.

BOW

Using D3 (3.25mm) crochet hook and B, make a 9-in (23-cm) crochet chain (see page 125).

TO MAKE UP HAT

Sew main hat seam. Tie crochet chain into a bow and stitch in place on the front of the hat using the photograph as a guide. Weave in all loose ends.

flip flop sandals

Using D3 (3.25mm) crochet hook and B, make two 2-in (5-cm) crochet chains (see page 125).

TO MAKE UP SANDALS

Sew the crochet chains in place on the feet so that they make a V-shape on top of the foot, using the photograph as a guide. Sew the two small fabric flowers in place. Weave in all loose ends.

beach bag

(MAKE 2)
Cast on 16 sts in B.
Row 1: K1, [p2, k1] to end.
Row 2: P1, [k2, p1] to end.
Row 3: Knit.
Row 4: Purl.
Rep rows 1–4, 5 times more.
Bind (cast) off.

HANDLES

Using D3 (3.25mm) crochet hook and D, make two 2½-in (6-cm) crochet chains (see page 125).

TO MAKE UP BAG

Sew sides and base of bag. Attach handles using the photograph as a guide. Attach fabric flower. Weave in all loose ends.

towel

(MAKE 1)
Cast on 22 sts in F.
Knit 4 rows.
Row 5: Knit.
Row 6: K2, p to last 2 sts, k2.
Rep rows 5–6, 29 times more.
Knit 4 rows.
Bind (cast) off.

TO MAKE UP TOWEL

Weave in all loose ends.

sunglasses

Using D3 (3.25mm) crochet hook and D, work one 5-in (13-cm) crochet chain and two ⅜-in (1-cm) chains (see page 125). Sew each yarn tail of the long chain to the center of the chain to create the eye frames. Sew the two short chains to the side for the arms. Weave in all loose ends except for those at the end of the arm pieces. Dip the glasses into a 50:50 solution of PVA glue and water, leaving the yarn tails at the end of the arms free. Squeeze lightly. Shape and leave to dry thoroughly on a piece of waxed paper or similar. Spread a thin layer of undiluted PVA on the back of the eye part of the frame and place on the acetate. Leave to dry thoroughly. Trim the acetate to fit. Use the yarn tails to sew the sunglasses in place.

Winter William

William's perfect day out is to wrap himself up in his favorite coat, hat, and scarf and wander through the park on a breezy day, with his loyal companion, Max the dachshund. Max loves eating, running, and digging; who knows what treasures lie lurking? And he loves cuddling and burrowing under blankets.

you will need

YARN AND MATERIALS

FOR DOLL

Debbie Bliss Baby Cashmerino (55% wool, 33% acrylic, 12% cashmere), 137yd (125m) per 1¾oz (50g) ball of sport weight (light DK) yarn
  ¾ ball of Teddy 308 (A)—head and body, arms, legs
  ¼ ball of Chocolate 11 (B)—hair
  ½ ball of Red 34 (C)—T-shirt, shoes
  ¼ ball of Denim 27 (D)—pants
  ¾ ball of Apple 02 (E)—duffel coat
  ¼ ball of Primrose 01 (F)—hat
  Small amount of Acid Yellow 91 (G)—scarf
  Very small amount of Black 300—eyes, nose, and mouth
  Very small amount of White 100—shoe laces

⁵⁄₁₆in (8mm) gray button

3 tiny wooden toggle buttons

1oz (30g) polyester toy filling

FOR DACHSHUND

Debbie Bliss Baby Cashmerino (55% wool, 33% acrylic, 12% cashmere), 137yd (125m) per 1¾oz (50g) ball of sport weight (light DK) yarn
  ¼ ball of Tobacco 98 (H)—dog
  Very small amounts of Black 300 and White 100—eyes
  Small amount of Sapphire 89 (J)—dog leash
Small amount of polyester toy filling

NEEDLES AND EQUIPMENT

US3 (3.25mm) knitting needles

D3 (3.25mm) crochet hook (or one of similar size)

Yarn sewing needle

Large-eyed embroidery needle

Coloring pencil in deep pink or red

GAUGE (TENSION)

Approximately 25 stitches and 34 rows to 4in (10cm) over st st (see also page 114)

ABBREVIATIONS

See page 127

main doll

Work as for basic pattern on page 9. Work head and body pieces, arms and legs in A.

HAIR

(MAKE 1)
Cast on 18 sts in B.
Work 6 rows in st st beg with a k row.
Row 7: Ssk, k to last 2 sts, k2tog. *(16 sts)*
Row 8: Purl.
Rep rows 7–8 twice more. *(12 sts)*
Row 13: Inc, k to last 2 sts, inc, k1. *(14 sts)*
Row 14: Purl.
Rep rows 13–14 once more. *(16 sts)*
Row 17: Inc, k3, bind (cast) off 8 sts, (1 st rem on needle from binding/casting off), k1, inc, k1. *(2 groups of 5 sts)*
Work on group of 5 sts just worked, leaving rem sts on needle.
Next row: P3, p2tog tbl. *(4 sts)*
Next row: Ssk, inc, k1.
Next row: P2, p2tog tbl. *(3 sts)*
Next row: Ssk, k1. *(2 sts)*
Next row: Purl.
Next row: K2tog. *(1 st)*
Fasten off.
Rejoin yarn to rem 5 sts on WS of work.
Next row: P2tog, p3. *(4 sts)*
Next row: Inc, k1, k2tog.
Next row: P2tog, p2. *(3 sts)*
Next row: K1, k2tog. *(2 sts)*
Next row: Purl.
Next row: K2tog. *(1 st)*
Fasten off.

TO MAKE UP DOLL

Make up main doll as explained on page 9. For eyes, work French knots (see page 124) using black yarn. Embroider mouth in straight stitch (see page 124) using embroidery floss (thread) or a separated strand of yarn. Work nose by working a couple of chain stitches (see page 124) in A, in a short vertical line. To make the nose slightly more prominent, work another couple of chain stitches over the ones you have just sewn. For the ears, work a few chain stitches in A, in a short

vertical line at the side of the head, in line with the eyes. Then work another row of chain stitches on top to make the ears a bit more prominent. Add a bit of color to the cheeks using the coloring pencil.
Seam the hair piece to form a cap shape. Pin then oversew (see page 125) the hair piece to head, using matching yarn.
Weave in all loose ends.

t-shirt

The T-shirt is knitted from the top down.
(MAKE 1)
Cast on 24 sts in C.
Row 1: Knit.
Row 2: K6, m1, k1, m1, k10, m1, k1, m1, k to end. *(28 sts)*
Row 3: K2, p to last 2 sts, k2.

Row 4: K6, m1, [k1, m1] 3 times, k10, m1, [k1, m1] 3 times, k to end. *(36 sts)*
Row 5: K2, p to last 2 sts, k2.
Row 6: K6, m1, k7, m1, k10, m1, k7, m1, k to end. *(40 sts)*
Row 7: K2, p to last 2 sts, k2.
Row 8: K6, m1, k1, m1, k7, m1, k1, m1, k10, m1, k1, m1, k7, m1, k1, m1, k to end. *(48 sts)*
Row 9: K2, p to last 2 sts, k2.
Row 10: K6, m1, k13, m1, k10, m1, k13, m1, k to end. *(52 sts)*
Row 11: K2, p to last 2 sts, k2.
Break yarn.
Row 12: Thread contrasting yarn through first 7 sts, rejoin yarn to RS of work and k13, turn and work on these 13 sts only, leaving rem sts on needle. Work 15 rows in st st beg with a p row.
Next row: Purl.
Bind (cast) off.
Put next 12 sts on contrasting yarn, knit 13 sts, then put rem 7 sts on contrasting yarn.

Turn and work on 13 sts just worked.
Work 15 rows in st st beg with a
p row.
Next row: Purl.
Bind (cast) off.
Put all 26 sts on yarn back on needle,
ready to work across all sts on RS
of work.
Next row: K6, [inc] twice, k10, [inc]
twice, k to end. *(30 sts)*
Work 14 rows in st st beg with a
p row.
Knit 2 rows.
Bind (cast) off.

TO MAKE UP T-SHIRT
Join the sleeve seams. Sew the back
seam of the T-shirt, from the lower
edge up to the base of the back
opening worked in garter stitch. Using
a yarn tail at the top of the back of the
T-shirt, use the crochet hook to work a
few crochet chains (see page 125).
Secure the free end of the chain to
form a button loop. Sew gray button
to corresponding side. Weave in all
loose ends.

pants

(MAKE 1)
Cast on 18 sts in D.
Row 1: Knit.
Work 26 rows in st st beg with a
k row.
Break yarn and leave sts on needle.
Cast on 18 sts on empty needle.
Row 1: Knit.
Work 26 rows in st st beg with a k row
but do not break yarn.
Now work across all 36 sts.
Work 13 rows in st st beg with a
k row.
Next row: [K1, p1] to end.
Rep last row once more.
Bind (cast) off keeping to the k1,
p1 patt.

TO MAKE UP PANTS
Sew inside leg and back seams.
Weave in all loose ends.

duffel coat

BACK AND FRONT
(MAKE 1)
Cast on 48 sts in E.
Knit 2 rows.
Row 3: Knit.
Row 4: K3, p to last 3 sts, k3.
Rep rows 3–4, 14 times more.
Row 33: K10, k2tog, turn.
Work on these 11 sts only, leaving rem
sts on needle.
Next row: P to last 3 sts, k3.
Next row: Knit.
Next row: P to last 3 sts, k3.
Rep last 2 rows twice more.
Next row: Knit.
Break yarn and rejoin it to rem 36 sts
on RS of work.
Next row: Ssk, k20, k2tog, turn.
Work on these 22 sts only, leaving rem
sts on needle.

Work 8 rows in st st beg with a p row.
Break yarn and rejoin it to rem 11 sts
on RS of work.
Next row: Ssk, k to end.
Next row: K3, p to end.
Rep last 2 rows 3 times more.
Next row: Knit.
Now work across all 44 sts.
Next row: K3, p to last 2 sts, k3.
Next row: K9, ssk, k2tog, k2, ssk,
k10, k2tog, k2, ssk, k2tog, k to end.
(38 sts)
Next row: Knit.
Next row: K6, [ssk] twice, [k2tog]
3 times, k6, [ssk] 3 times, [k2tog]
twice, k to end. *(28 sts)*
Next row: Knit.
Bind (cast) off.

SLEEVES

(MAKE 2)

Cast on 16 sts in E.

Knit 2 rows.

Work 18 rows in st st beg with a k row.

Bind (cast) off.

HOOD

(MAKE 1)

Cast on 36 sts in E.

Knit 2 rows.

Work 12 rows in st st beg with a k row.

Row 15: K13, ssk, k6, k2tog, k to end. *(34 sts)*

Row 16: Purl.

Row 17: K13, ssk, k4, k2tog, k to end. *(32 sts)*

Row 18: Purl.

Row 19: K13, ssk, k2, k2tog, k to end. *(30 sts)*

Row 20: Purl.

Bind (cast) off.

POCKET

(MAKE 2)

Cast on 8 sts in E.

Row 1: Knit.

Work 7 rows in st st beg with a k row.

Bind (cast) off.

TO MAKE UP COAT

Fold hood in half widthwise and seam bound- (cast-) off edges together, so that cast-on edge forms front of hood, near face. Stitch hood to neck edge of coat. Join sleeve seams. Insert sleeves into coat and oversew (see page 125) top of sleeve to armholes from the inside. Oversew pockets in place. Sew on toggles. You can use the gaps between the knitted stitches for buttonholes for the toggles.

hat

MAIN HAT

(MAKE 1)

Cast on 36 sts in F.

Work 14 rows in st st beg with a k row.

Row 15: [K2tog] to end. *(18 sts)*

Row 16: Purl.

Row 17: [K2tog] to end. *(9 sts)*

Row 18: [P2tog] twice, p1, [p2tog] twice. *(5 sts)*

Break yarn, thread through rem sts, and secure.

EARS

(MAKE 2)

Cast on 4 sts in F.

Work 2 rows in st st beg with a k row.

Row 3: Ssk, k2tog. *(2 sts)*

Row 4: P2tog. *(1 st)*

Row 5: Inc. *(2 sts)*

Row 6: [Inc pwise] twice. *(4 sts)*

Work 2 rows in st st beg with a k row.

Bind (cast) off.

TO MAKE UP HAT

Sew main hat seam. Fold ear piece in half so that right sides are on the inside. Oversew (see page 125) around curved edges. Turn piece the right way out and stitch in place on the main hat using the photograph as a guide.

scarf

(MAKE 1)

Cast on 4 sts in G.

Knit 108 rows.

Bind (cast) off.

TO MAKE UP SCARF

Weave in all loose ends.

shoes

(MAKE 2)

Cast on 26 sts in C.

Work 4 rows in st st beg with a k row.

Row 5: K7, [ssk] 3 times, [k2tog] 3 times, k to end. *(20 sts)*

Row 6: Purl.

Row 7: K6, [ssk] twice, [k2tog] twice, k to end. *(16 sts)*

Row 8: Knit.

Bind (cast) off.

TO MAKE UP SHOES

Fold shoe pieces in half so that the right side is on the inside and oversew (see page 125) sole. Turn the pieces the right way out and sew the back seams. Using white yarn, work two straight stitches (see page 124) on front of shoes to represent laces. Weave in all loose ends.

dachshund

BODY AND HEAD
(MAKE 1)

Cast on 12 sts in H.

Row 1: Inc, k to last 2 sts, inc, k1. *(14 sts)*

Row 2: Purl.

Rep rows 1–2 once more. *(16 sts)*

Work 8 rows in st st beg with a k row.

Row 13: K8, turn and cast on 8 sts for back of head, turn back and k to end. *(24 sts)*

Work 3 rows in st st beg with a p row.

Row 17: K1, ssk, k to last 3 sts, k2tog, k1. *(22 sts)*

Row 18: Purl.

Row 19: Bind (cast) off 5 sts, k to end. *(17 sts)*

Row 20: Bind (cast) off 5 sts pwise, p to end. *(12 sts)*

Row 21: Bind (cast) off 2 sts, k to end. *(10 sts)*

Row 22: Bind (cast) off 2 sts pwise, p to end. *(8 sts)*

Row 23: K1, ssk, k2, k2tog, k1. *(6 sts)*

Break yarn, thread through rem sts, and secure.

FRONT LEGS
(MAKE 2)

Cast on 6 sts in H.

Work 8 rows in st st beg with a k row. Break yarn, thread through sts, and secure.

BACK LEGS
(MAKE 2)

Cast on 6 sts in H.

Work 2 rows in st st beg with a k row.

Row 3: K1, m1, k to last st, m1, k1. *(8 sts)*

Row 4: Purl.

Rep rows 3–4 once more. *(10 sts)*

Work 2 rows in st st beg with a k row.

Row 9: K1, ssk, k to last 3 sts, k2tog, k1. *(8 sts)*

Row 10: P2tog, p to last 2 sts, p2tog tbl. *(6 sts)*

Bind (cast) off.

EARS
(MAKE 2)

Cast on 3 sts in H.

Knit 7 rows.

Row 8: Sl1, k2tog, p2sso. *(1 st)*

Fasten off.

TAIL

Using crochet hook and H, work a ½-in (1.5-cm) crochet chain (see page 125).

TO MAKE UP DACHSHUND

Fold head and body piece in half so that the right sides are facing outward. Sew seam that forms back of neck. Sew lower seam, leaving opening on lower side of body for stuffing. Stuff and close gap. Fold back legs in half and seam, stuffing as you go. Do the same for the front legs. Stitch limbs in place. Sew ears in place. Stitch the tail in place. For eyes, work two French knots (see page 124) using a separated strand of black yarn. Using a separated strand of white yarn, work a circle of chain stitches (see page 124) around the French knots. Using a separated strand of black yarn, work a small circle of chain stitches for the nose. Add a vertical straight stitch (see page 124) beneath the nose. Weave in all loose ends.

DOG LEASH

Using crochet hook and J, make an 11-in (28-cm) crochet chain (see page 125). Secure one end around the dog's neck and make a loop at the other end for the handle.

Girls' Night Gretel

When the weekend comes around, Gretel is more than ready for a great night out. She loves a disco, a karaoke evening, or just pizza with friends. She spends ages choosing the right outfit, doing her hair, and selecting the perfect jewelry. Then she packs a few essentials into her clutch purse and she's ready to go.

main doll

Work as for basic pattern on page 9. Work head and body pieces, arms and legs in A.

HAIR
(MAKE 1)
Cast on 19 sts in B.
Row 1: K1, [p1, k1] to end.
Rep row 1, 3 times more.
Row 5: P2tog, [k1, p1] to last 3 sts, k1, p2tog tbl. (17 sts)
Row 6: P1, [k1, p1] to end.
Row 7: Ssk, [p1, k1] to last 3 sts, p1, k2tog. (15 sts)
Row 8: K1, [p1, k1] to end.
Rep rows 5–6 once more. (13 sts)
Row 11: Inc pwise, [k1, p1] to last 2 sts, k1, inc pwise. (15 sts)
Row 12: K1, [p1, k1] to end.
Row 13: Inc, [p1, k1] to last 2 sts, p1, inc. (17 sts)
Row 14: P1, [k1, p1] to end.
Row 15: Inc pwise, [k1, p1] twice, bind (cast) off 7 sts, keeping to the k1, p1 patt, (1 st rem on needle from binding/casting off) k1, p1, k1, inc pwise. (2 groups of 6 sts)
Work on last group of 6 sts only, leaving rem sts on needle.
Next row: [K1, p1] twice, ssk. (5 sts)
Next row: P2tog, k1, p1, inc.
Next row: P1, k1, p1, k2tog. (4 sts)
Next row: P2tog, k1, p1. (3 sts)

Next row: Sl 1, k2tog, psso. (1 st)
Fasten off.
Rejoin yarn to rem sts on WS of work.
Next row: K2tog, [p1, k1] twice. (5 sts)
Next row: Inc, p1, k1, p2tog.
Next row: K2tog, p1, k1, p1. (4 sts)
Next row: P1, k1, p2tog. (3 sts)
Next row: K3tog. (1 st)
Fasten off.

BUN
Cast on 4 sts in B.
Row 1: [Inc] 4 times. (8 sts)
Row 2: Knit.
Row 3: [Inc] 8 times. (16 sts)
Knit 3 rows.
Row 7: [K2tog] 8 times. (8 sts)
Row 8: [K2tog] 4 times. (4 sts)
Break yarn and thread through rem sts.

TO MAKE UP DOLL
Make up main doll as explained on page 9.
For eyes, work French knots (see page 124) using B. Embroider mouth in straight stitch (see page 124) using embroidery floss (thread) or a separated strand of yarn. Work nose by working a couple of chain stitches (see page 124) in A, in a short vertical line. To make the nose slightly more prominent, work another couple of chain stitches over the ones you have

you will need

YARN AND MATERIALS
Debbie Bliss Baby Cashmerino (55% wool, 33% acrylic, 12% cashmere), 137yd (125m) per 1¾oz (50g) ball of sport weight (light DK) yarn
  ¾ ball of Teddy 308 (A)—head and body, arms, legs
  ¼ ball of Black 300 (B)—hair, eyes
  ½ ball of Acid Yellow 91 (C)—dress
  ¼ ball of Orange 92 (D)—bolero
  Small amount of Primrose 01 (E)—underpants
  ¼ ball of Mint 03 (F)—shoes, clutch purse
  Very small amount of Drake 302 yarn—necklace

Very small amount of coral, red, or pink embroidery floss (thread) or yarn—mouth

2 x very small readymade pale yellow ribbon bows for shoes

Small lime green button for back of dress

Small orange button for clutch purse

17 x ³⁄₁₆in (4mm) pearl beads

2 x small silver beads

1oz (30g) polyester toy filling

NEEDLES AND EQUIPMENT
US3 (3.25mm) knitting needles

D3 (3.25mm) crochet hook (or one of similar size)

Yarn sewing needle

Large-eyed embroidery needle

Pins

Coloring pencil in deep pink or red

GAUGE (TENSION)
Approximately 25 stitches and 34 rows to 4in (10cm) over st st (see also page 114)

ABBREVIATIONS
See page 127

just sewn. For the ears, work a few chain stitches in A, in a short vertical line at the side of the head, in line with the eyes. Then work another row of chain stitches on top to make the ears a bit more prominent. Stitch silver beads in place for earrings, using the photograph as a guide. Add a bit of color to the cheeks using the coloring pencil.

Seam the hair piece to form a cap shape. Pin then oversew (see page 125) the hair piece to head, using matching yarn. For bun, run yarn tail around the outside of the knitted pieces, very close to the edge. Pull up into a small sphere shape, stuffing with a small piece of filling as you go. Stitch in place on top of the head. Weave in all loose ends.

dress

The dress is knitted from the top down.
(MAKE 1)
Cast on 24 sts in C.
Row 1: K6, m1, k1, m1, k10, m1, k1, m1, k to end. *(28 sts)*
Row 2: K6, m1, k3, m1, k10, m1, k3, m1, k to end. *(32 sts)*
Row 3: K6, p5, k10, p5, k to end.

Row 4: K6, m1, k5, m1, k10, m1, k5, m1, k to end. *(36 sts)*
Row 5: K6, p7, k10, p7, k to end.
Row 6: K6, m1, k7, m1, k10, m1, k7, m1, k to end. *(40 sts)*
Row 7: K6, p9, k10, p9, k to end.
Row 8: K6, m1, k9, m1, k10, m1, k9, m1, k to end. *(44 sts)*
Row 9: K6, p11, k10, p11, k to end.
Knit 2 rows.
Row 12: K6, bind (cast) off 11 sts, (1 st rem on needle from binding/casting off) k9, bind (cast) off 11 sts, k to end. *(22 sts)*
Row 13: K2, [m1, k2] twice, turn and cast on 2 sts, turn back, [k2, m1] twice, [k1, m1] twice, k2, m1, k2, turn and cast on 2 sts, turn back, [k2, m1] twice, k2. *(35 sts)*
Row 14: K5, [p1, k5] to end.
Row 15: K1, [p3, k3] to last 4 sts, p3, k1.
Row 16: P2, [k1, p2] to end.
Row 17: P1, [k3, p3] to last 4 sts, k3, p1.
Row 18: K2, [p1, k5] to last 3 sts, p1, k2.
Row 19: Purl.
Rep rows 14–19 (last 6 rows) 5 times more.
Row 50: Knit.
Row 51: Purl.
Bind (cast) off pwise (on RS of work).

TO MAKE UP DRESS

Sew the back seam of the dress, leaving a gap at the top so the dress will fit over the doll's head. Using a yarn tail at the top of the back of the dress, use the crochet hook to work a few crochet chains (see page 125). Secure the free end of the chain to form a button loop. Sew lime green button to corresponding side. Weave in all loose ends.

bolero

(MAKE 1)
Cast on 20 sts in D.
Row 1: Knit.
Work 4 rows in st st beg with a k row.
Row 6: K2, m1, k to last 2 sts, m1, k2. *(22 sts)*
Row 7: Purl.
Rep rows 6–7 twice more. *(26 sts)*
Row 12: Cast on 4 sts, k to end. *(30 sts)*
Row 13: Cast on 4 sts, p to end. *(34 sts)*
Rep rows 12–13 once more. *(42 sts)*
Work 6 rows in st st beg with a k row.
Row 22: K15, bind (cast) off 12 sts, k to end. *(30 sts in 2 groups of 15 sts)*
Work on first group of 15 sts only, leaving rem sts on needle.
Next row: Purl.

Next row: K2, m1, k to end. *(16 sts)*
Next row: Purl.
Rep last 2 rows 3 times more. *(19 sts)*
Next row: K2, m1, k to end. *(20 sts)*
Next row: Bind (cast) off 4 sts pwise, p to end. *(16 sts)*
Next row: Knit.
Rep last 2 rows once more. *(12 sts)*
Next row: Purl.
Next row: K to last 4 sts, k2tog, k2. *(11 sts)*
Next row: Purl.
Rep last 2 rows twice more. *(9 sts)*
Next row: Knit.
Next row: Purl.
Next row: K2, ssk, k to end. *(8 sts)*
Next row: Knit.
Bind (cast) off.
Rejoin yarn to rem sts on WS of work.
Next row: Purl.
Next row: K to last 2 sts, m1, k2. *(16 sts)*
Next row: Purl.
Rep last 2 rows 4 times more. *(20 sts)*
Next row: Bind (cast) off 4 sts, k to end. *(16 sts)*
Next row: Purl.
Rep last 2 rows once more. *(12 sts)*
Next row: K2, k2tog, k to end. *(11 sts)*
Next row: Purl.
Rep last 2 rows twice more. *(9 sts)*
Next row: Knit.
Next row: Purl.
Next row: K2, k2tog, k to end. *(8 sts)*
Next row: Knit.
Bind (cast) off.
With RS of work facing, pick up and knit 18 sts from one lower edge of bolero front to neck edge, 12 sts across neck, and 18 sts from neck to second lower edge.
Bind (cast) off kwise.

TO MAKE UP BOLERO
Sew sleeve and side seams. Weave in all loose ends.

underpants

(MAKE 1)
Cast on 16 sts in E.
Knit 2 rows.
Break yarn and cast on another 16 sts on the same needle.
Knit 2 rows.
Now knit across all 32 sts.
Work 8 rows in st st beg with a k row.
Next row: [K1, p1] to end.
Rep last row once more.
Bind (cast) off keeping to the k1, p1 patt.

TO MAKE UP UNDERPANTS
Join inside leg and back seams.
Weave in all loose ends.

shoes
(MAKE 2)
Cast on 24 sts in F.
Work 4 rows in st st beg with a k row.
Row 5: K6, [ssk] 3 times, [k2tog] 3 times, k to end. *(18 sts)*
Bind (cast) off pwise.

TO MAKE UP SHOES
Fold shoe piece in half so that the right side is on the inside and oversew (see page 125) sole. Turn the piece the right way out and sew the back seam using mattress stitch (see page 126). Sew bows in place. Weave in all loose ends.

clutch purse

(MAKE 1)
Cast on 12 sts in F.
Knit 28 rows.
Row 29: K1, ssk, k to last 3 sts, k2tog, k1. *(10 sts)*
Row 30: Knit.
Row 31: K1, ssk, k to last 3 sts, k2tog, k1. *(8 sts)*
Bind (cast) off pwise.

WRIST STRAP
(MAKE 1)
Using crochet hook and F, make a 3-in (8-cm) chain (see page 125).

TO MAKE UP PURSE
Fold piece into purse shape using the photo as a guide and sew side seams. Sew on wrist strap and orange button. A gap between the knitted stitches can be used for buttonhole. Weave in all loose ends.

necklace

Thread pearl beads onto length of Drake 302 yarn, making a knot in the yarn between each bead. Tie knots after the end beads to keep all the beads in place. Make a knot at each end of the yarn before tying the necklace around the doll's neck.

Traditional Tina

Some girls love slinky party dresses, sparkly stuff, and fancy hairstyles, but Tina is a bit different. She's much happier in practical clothes and wears her hair in simple braids. Today she's chosen a pleated skirt, her favorite rabbit sweater, and sensible shoes.

you will need

YARN AND MATERIALS

Debbie Bliss Baby Cashmerino (55% wool, 33% acrylic, 12% cashmere), 137yd (125m) per 1¾oz (50g) ball of sport weight (light DK) yarn

½ ball of Clotted Cream 65 (A)—head and body, arms
¼ ball of Primrose 01 (B)—legs
¼ ball of Acid Yellow 91 (C)—hair
½ ball of Duck Egg 26 (D)—sweater
Small amount of White 100 (E)—rabbit motif on sweater
¼ ball of Coral 86 (F)—skirt
Small amount of Baby Pink 601 (G)—underpants
Small amount of Royal 70 (H)—shoes
Very small amount of Black 300—eyes and rabbit features

Very small amount of coral, red, or pink embroidery floss (thread) or yarn—mouth

2 x 8-in (20-cm) lengths of ³⁄₁₆in (4mm) red ribbon

1oz (30g) polyester toy filling

NEEDLES AND EQUIPMENT

US3 (3.25mm) knitting needles

D3 (3.25mm) crochet hook (or one of similar size)

J10 (6mm) crochet hook (or one of similar size)

Yarn sewing needle

Large-eyed embroidery needle

Coloring pencil in deep pink or red

4 stitch markers or small safety pins

GAUGE (TENSION)

Approximately 25 stitches and 34 rows to 4in (10cm) over st st (see also page 114)

ABBREVIATIONS

See page 127

main doll

Work as for basic pattern on page 9.
Work head and body pieces and arms
in A.
Work legs in B.

HAIR

(MAKE 1)
Cast on 18 sts in C.
Work 4 rows in st st beg with a k row.
Row 5: Ssk, k to last 2 sts, k2tog.
(16 sts)
Row 6: Purl.
Rep last 2 rows twice more. *(12 sts)*
Row 11: Inc, k to last 2 sts, inc, k1.
(14 sts)
Row 12: Purl.
Rep last 2 rows twice more. *(18 sts)*
Row 17: K4, bind (cast) off 10 sts,
k to end. *(2 groups of 4 sts)*
Work on 4 sts just worked only, leaving
rem sts on needle.
Next row: Purl.

Next row: Ssk, k to end. *(3 sts)*
Next row: P1, p2tog tbl. *(2 sts)*
Next row: Ssk. *(1 st)*
Fasten off.
Rejoin yarn to rem 4 sts on WS
of work.
Next row: Purl.
Next row: K to last 2 sts, k2tog.
(3 sts)
Next row: P2tog, p1. *(2 sts)*
Next row: K2tog. *(1 st)*
Fasten off.

BRAIDS (PLAITS)

(MAKE 2)
Using J10 (6mm) crochet hook and
C trebled, make two 2¾-in (7-cm)
crochet chains (see page 125). Fasten
off leaving long ends.

TO MAKE UP DOLL

Make up main doll as explained on
page 9. For eyes, work French knots
(see page 124) using black yarn.
Embroider mouth in straight stitch (see
page 124) using embroidery floss
(thread) or a separated strand of yarn.
Work nose by working a couple of
chain stitches (see page 124) in A, in a
short vertical line. To make the nose
slightly more prominent, work another
couple of chain stitches over the
ones you have just sewn. Add a bit
of color to the cheeks using the
coloring pencil.
Seam the hair piece and to form a cap
shape. Pin then oversew (see page
125) the hair piece to head, using
matching yarn. Stitch braids (plaits) in
place at the side of the head, using
photograph as a guide. Weave in all
loose ends. Tie the ribbon round the
ends of the braids (plaits), and trim
and separate strands of yarn below.

sweater

FRONT
(MAKE 1)
Cast on 7 sts in D, 8 sts in E, 7 sts in D. *(22 sts)*
Row 1: Knit in colors as set.
Work 8 rows in st st keeping to colors as set, beg with a k row.
Row 10: K7 in D, k2 in E, k4 in D, k2 in E, k in D to end.
Work 7 rows in st st keeping to the colors as set, beg with a p row.
Break all but leading D yarn.
Work 2 rows in st st beg with a k row.
*Row 20: K2, ssk, k to last 4 sts, k2tog, k2. *(20 sts)*
Mark beg and end of last row with stitch markers or small safety pins.
Row 21: Purl.
Rep rows 20–21 once more. *(18 sts)*
Work 6 rows in st st beg with a k row.
Row 30: Bind (cast) off 3 sts, k to end. *(15 sts)*
Row 31: Bind (cast) off 3 sts pwise, p to end. *(12 sts)*
Work 4 rows in st st beg with a k row.
Bind (cast) off loosely.

BACK
(MAKE 1)
Cast on 22 sts in D.
Row 1: Knit.
Work 18 rows in st st beg with a k row.
Work as for front from * to end.

SLEEVES
Join neck edges and shoulders of front and back pieces. With RS facing and D, pick up and knit 8 sts from one stitch marker or safety pin to shoulder edges and another 8 sts from shoulder edges to second stitch marker or safety pin. Work 21 rows in st st beg with a p row. Bind (cast) off loosely. Rep for second sleeve.

TO MAKE UP SWEATER
Join side and sleeve seams. Weave in all loose ends. For eyes work French knots (see page 124) and for mouth embroider a cross using black yarn.

skirt

(MAKE 1)
Cast on 51 sts in F.
Row 1: K3, [p1, k3] to end.
Row 2: P3, [k1, p3] to end.
Rep rows 1–2, 9 times more.
Row 21: K3, [p1, k3] to end.
Row 22: [Sl2, k1, p2sso, k1] to last 3 sts, sl2, k1, p2sso. *(25 sts)*
Row 23: Knit.
Bind (cast) off.

TO MAKE UP SKIRT
Join back seam. Weave in all loose ends.

underpants

(MAKE 1)
Cast on 16 sts in G.
Knit 2 rows.
Break yarn and cast on another 16 sts on the same needle.
Knit 2 rows.
Now work across all 32 sts.
Work 8 rows in st st beg with a k row.
Next row: [K1, p1] to end.
Rep last row once more.
Bind (cast) off keeping to the k1, p1 patt.

TO MAKE UP UNDERPANTS
Join inside leg and back seams. Weave in all loose ends.

shoes

(MAKE 2)
Cast on 24 sts in H.
Work 4 rows in st st beg with a k row.
Row 5: K6, [ssk] 3 times, [k2tog] 3 times, k to end. *(18 sts)*
Bind (cast) off pwise.

STRAPS
(MAKE 2)
Using D3 (3.25mm) crochet hook and H, work two ½in (1.25cm) crochet chains (see page 125).

TO MAKE UP SHOES
Fold shoe piece in half so that the right side is on the inside and oversew (see page 125) sole. Turn the piece the right way out and sew the back seam using mattress stitch (see page 126). Sew straps in place, using the photograph as a guide. Weave in all loose ends.

Pete's more of a fancy-dress pirate than a villain from the high seas, and he's more concerned with looking good than scaring people. With his red and black striped pants and bandana he certainly looks the part. And he's particularly proud of that gold buckle on his belt, so please don't forget it!

YARN AND MATERIALS

Debbie Bliss Baby Cashmerino (55% wool, 33% acrylic, 12% cashmere), 137yd (125m) per 1¾oz (50g) ball of sport weight (light DK) yarn

- ¾ ball Clotted Cream 65 (A)—head and body, arms, legs
- ¼ ball Tobacco 98 (B)—hair
- ½ ball White 100 (C)—shirt
- ¼ ball Sea Green 99 (D)—vest (waistcoat)
- ¼ ball Red 34 (E)—pants, bandana hat
- ½ ball Black 300 (F)—pants, belt, boots, eyes

⁵⁄₁₆in (8mm) brass ring

Very small amount of gold metallic yarn or embroidery floss—belt buckle

Very small amount of coral, red, or pink embroidery floss (thread) or yarn—mouth

1oz (30g) polyester toy filling

NEEDLES AND EQUIPMENT

US3 (3.25mm) knitting needles

Yarn sewing needle

Large-eyed embroidery needle

2 stitch markers or small safety pins

Pins

Coloring pencil in deep pink or red

GAUGE (TENSION)

Approximately 25 stitches and 34 rows to 4in (10cm) over st st (see also page 114)

ABBREVIATIONS

See page 127

main doll

Work as for basic pattern on page 9. Work head and body pieces, arms and legs in A.

HAIR

(MAKE 1)

Cast on 18 sts in B.

Work 4 rows in st st beg with a k row.

Row 5: Ssk, k to last 2 sts, k2tog. (16 sts)

Row 6: Purl.

Rep last 2 rows twice more. (12 sts)

Row 11: Inc, k to last 2 sts, inc, k1. (14 sts)

Row 12: Purl.

Rep last 2 rows twice more. (18 sts)

Row 15: K4, bind (cast) off 10 sts, k to end. (2 groups of 4 sts)

Work on 4 sts just worked only, leaving rem sts on needle.

Next row: Purl.

Next row: Ssk, k to end. (3 sts)

Next row: P1, p2tog tbl. (2 sts)

Next row: Ssk. (1 st)

Fasten off.

Rejoin yarn to rem 4 sts on WS of work.

Next row: Purl.

Next row: K to last 2 sts, k2tog. (3 sts)

Next row: P2tog, p1. (2 sts)

Next row: K2tog. (1 st)

Fasten off.

TO MAKE UP DOLL

Make up main doll as explained on page 9.

For eyes, work French knots (see page 124) using F. Embroider mouth in straight stitch (see page 124) using embroidery floss (thread) or a separated strand of yarn. Work nose by working a couple of chain stitches (see page 124) in A, in a short vertical line. To make the nose slightly more prominent, work another couple of chain stitches over the ones you have just sewn. For the ears, work a few chain stitches in A, in a short vertical line at the side of the head, in line with the eyes. Then work another row of chain stitches on top to make the ears a bit more prominent. Sew the brass ring in place for the earring. Add a bit of color to the cheeks using the coloring pencil.

Seam the hair piece to form a cap shape. Pin then oversew (see page 125) the hair piece to the head, using matching yarn.

Weave in all loose ends.

shirt

(MAKE 1)
Cast on 40 sts in C.
Row 1: Knit.
Work 18 rows in st st beg with a
k row.
Row 20: K10, turn. Leave rem sts on
needle and work on 10 sts just knitted.
Work 6 rows in st st beg with a p row.
Break yarn and rejoin it to rem 30 sts
on RS of work.
Next row: K20, turn. Leave rem
sts on needle and work on 20 sts
just knitted.
Next row: P8, k4, p to end.
Next row: K10, turn and work on
these 10 sts only, leaving rem sts
on needle.
Next row: K2, p to end.
Next row: Knit.
Rep last 2 rows once more.
Break yarn and rejoin it to the 10 rem
sts forming second front side, on RS
of work.
Next row: Knit.
Next row: P to last 2 sts, k2.
Next row: Knit.
Rep last 2 rows once more.
Break yarn and rejoin it to rem 10 sts
on RS of work.
Work 7 rows in st st beg with a k row.
Next row: K20, turn and work
on these sts only, leaving rem sts
on needle.
Next row: K6, [ssk] twice, [k2tog]
twice, k to end. (16 sts)
Next row: Knit.

Next row: K6, ssk, k2tog, k to end.
(14 sts)
Knit 5 rows.
Bind (cast) off.
Rejoin yarn to rem 20 sts on WS
of work.
Next row: Knit.
Next row: K6, [ssk] twice, [k2tog]
twice, k to end. (16 sts)
Next row: Knit.
Next row: K6, ssk, k2tog, k to end.
(14 sts)
Knit 5 rows.
Bind (cast) off.

SLEEVES
(MAKE 2)
Cast on 14 sts in C.
Knit 4 rows.
Work 18 rows in st st beg with a
k row.
Bind (cast) off.

TO MAKE UP SHIRT
Sew back seam and sleeve seams.
Insert sleeves into armholes and stitch
in place from the inside. Weave in all
loose ends.

vest (waistcoat)

Cast on 36 sts in D.
Row 1: Knit.
Row 2: Knit.
Row 3: K2, p to last 2 sts, k2.
Rep rows 2–3, 4 times more.
Row 12: Knit.

Row 13: K2, p5, k4, p14, k4, p5, k2.
Row 14: K9, turn and work on 9 sts
just worked only, leaving rem sts
on needle.
Next row: K2, p5, k2.
Next row: Knit.
Rep last 2 rows 3 times more.
Break yarn and rejoin it to rem 27 sts
on RS of work.
Next row: K18, turn and work on
18 sts just worked only, leaving rem
sts on needle.
Next row: K2, p to last 2 sts, k2.
Next row: Knit.
Next row: K2, p to last 2 sts, k2.
Next row: K4, ssk, k6, k2tog, k4.
(16 sts)
Next row: K2, p to last 2 sts, k2.
Next row: K4, ssk, k4, k2tog, k4.
(14 sts)
Next row: K2, p to last 2 sts, k2.
Next row: Knit.
Break yarn and rejoin it to rem 9 sts on
RS of work.
Next row: Knit.
Next row: K2, p to last 2 sts, k2.
Next row: Knit.
Rep last 2 rows 3 times more.
Now work across all 32 sts.
Next row: K2, p5, k4, p10, k4,
p5, k2.
Knit 4 rows.
Bind (cast) off.

TO MAKE UP VEST (WAISTCOAT)
Weave in all loose ends.

pants

(MAKE 2)
Cast on 28 sts in E, marking 11th st
with a stitch marker or small safety pin.
Work 2 rows in st st beg with a k row.
Leave E at side and join in F.
Work 2 rows in st st beg with a k row.
Rep last 4 rows 4 times more.
Break F.
Work 2 rows in st st in E beg with a
k row.
Bind (cast) off, marking 11th st with a
stitch marker or small safety pin.

WAISTBAND

Join cast-on edge of one of the pieces with bound- (cast-) off edge of the other from 11th stitches upward to form front crotch seam.
With RS facing and F, pick up and k 35 sts across waist edge.
Row 1: K1, [p1, k1] to end.
Row 2: P1, [k1, p1] to end.
Row 3: K1, [p1, k1] to end.
Bind (cast) off.

ANKLE CUFFS

With RS facing and F, pick up and k 17 sts across ankle edge of pants.
Knit 1 row
Bind (cast) off.
Rep for second ankle cuff.

TO MAKE UP PANTS

Sew inside leg and back seams.
Weave in all loose ends.

bandana hat

MAIN HAT

(MAKE 1)
Cast on 36 sts in E.
Row 1: Knit.
Work 8 rows in st st beg with a k row.
Row 10: [K2tog] to end. *(18 sts)*
Row 11: Purl.
Row 12: [K2tog] to end. *(9 sts)*

Row 13: [P2tog] twice, p1, [p2tog] twice. *(5 sts)*
Break yarn, thread through rem sts, and secure.

KNOT

(MAKE 1)
Cast on 16 sts in E.
Row 1: Knit.
Bind (cast) off.

TO MAKE UP HAT

Sew main seam of hat. Tie strip for knot in a single knot. Secure knot to side of hat, at the bottom of seam.

belt

(MAKE 1)
Cast on 46 sts in F.
Row 1: Knit.
Bind (cast) off.

TO MAKE UP BELT

Join belt piece into a circle so that the short edges overlap and one of the short edges forms the free end of the belt. Using gold metallic yarn or embroidery floss (thread), work a square in chain stitch (see page 124) for the belt buckle.

boots

(MAKE 2)
Cast on 26 sts in F.
Row 1: Knit.
Row 2: Purl.
Row 3: Knit.
Rep rows 1–3 once more.
Row 7: Purl.
Row 8: K7, [ssk] 3 times, [k2tog] 3 times, k to end. *(20 sts)*
Row 9: Purl.
Row 10: K6, [ssk] twice, [k2tog] twice, k to end. *(16 sts)*
Work 3 rows in st st beg with a p row.
Row 14: K2, m1, k to last 2 sts, m1, k2. *(18 sts)*
Work 5 rows in st st beg with a p row.
Row 20: K2, m1, k to last 2 sts, m1, k2. *(20 sts)*
Row 21: Purl.
Knit 2 rows.
Bind (cast) off loosely.

TO MAKE UP BOOTS

Fold boot pieces in half so that the right side is on the inside and oversew (see page 125) sole. Turn the pieces the right way out and sew the back seams. Weave in all loose ends.

Festival Chic Fiona

Fiona loves music, clothes, jewelry, and camping, so it's no surprise that she loves a summer music festival. Whether it's tapping her feet to the beat, sinking her teeth into a street food snack, or taking part in a late-night talkfest, Fiona is in her element. And with her stout purple boots, she doesn't even care if it rains.

you will need

YARN AND MATERIALS

Debbie Bliss Baby Cashmerino (55% wool, 33% acrylic, 12% cashmere), 137yd (125m) per 1¾oz (50g) ball of sport weight (light DK) yarn
- ¾ ball of Teddy 308 (A)—head and body, arms, legs
- ¼ ball of Black 300 (B)—hair, eyes, soles of boots
- ¼ ball of Baby Pink 601 (C)—top
- ¼ ball of Lipstick Pink 78 (D)—vest (waistcoat)
- ¼ ball of Baby Blue 204 (E)—shorts
- ¼ ball of Cyclamen 95 (F)—boots
- ¼ ball of Sapphire 89 (G)—purse and hairband
- Small amount of Mint 03 (H)—purse strap
- Very small amount of Ecru 101—necklace

Very small amount of coral, red, or pink embroidery floss (thread) or yarn—mouth

2 x ½in (13mm) brass rings

⅜in (10mm) green button

18 small multi-colored wooden beads

Small brass Hamsa hand charm

1oz (30g) polyester toy filling

NEEDLES AND EQUIPMENT

US3 (3.25mm) knitting needles

D3 (3.25mm) crochet hook (or one of similar size)

J10 (6mm) crochet hook (or one of similar size)

Yarn sewing needle

Large-eyed embroidery needle

Stitch holder

Pins

Coloring pencil in deep pink or red

GAUGE (TENSION)

Approximately 25 stitches and 34 rows to 4in (10cm) over st st (see also page 114)

ABBREVIATIONS

See page 127

main doll

Work as for basic pattern on page 9. Work head and body pieces, arms and legs in A.

HAIR
(MAKE 1)
Cast on 19 sts in B.
Row 1: K1, [p1, k1] to end.

Rep row 1, 4 times more.
Cast on 19 sts, bind (cast) off 22 sts.
*Transfer rem st from right-hand to left-hand needle.
Cast on 19 sts, bind (cast) off 22 sts.**
Rep from * to ** 4 times.
Transfer rem st from right-hand to left-hand needle.
Cast on 19 sts, bind (cast) off.
Fasten off.
Pick up and k 19 sts along long side of

main hair piece and work a corresponding fringe along this side.
Cast on 19 sts, bind (cast) off 22 sts.
*Transfer rem st from right-hand to left-hand needle.
Cast on 19 sts, bind (cast) off 22 sts.**
Rep from * to ** 4 times.
Transfer rem st from right-hand to left-hand needle.
Cast on 19 sts, bind (cast) off.
Fasten off.

TO MAKE UP DOLL

Make up main doll as explained on page 9. For eyes, work French knots (see page 124) using B. Embroider mouth in straight stitch (see page 124) using embroidery floss (thread) or a separated strand of yarn. Work nose by working a couple of chain stitches (see page 124) in A, in a short vertical line. To make the nose slightly more prominent, work another couple of chain stitches over the ones you have just sewn. For the ears, work a few chain stitches in A, in a short vertical line at the side of the head, in line with the eyes. Then work another row of chain stitches on top to make the ears a bit more prominent. Stitch brass rings in place for earrings using the photograph as a guide. Add a bit of color to the cheeks using the coloring pencil.

Stretch hair piece over top seam of head from one ear to the other. Pin then stitch in place.

top

(MAKE 1)
Cast on 18 sts in C.
Row 1: Knit.
Work 2 rows in st st beg with a k row.
Row 4: K2, m1, k to last 2 sts, m1, k2. *(20 sts)*
Row 5: Purl.
Rep rows 4–5 twice more. *(24 sts)*
Row 10: Cast on 4 sts, k to end. *(28 sts)*
Row 11: Cast on 4 sts, p to end. *(32 sts)*
Rep rows 10–11 once more. *(40 sts)*
Work 4 rows in st st beg with a k row.
Row 18: K14, bind (cast) off 12 sts pwise, k to end. *(28 sts in 2 groups of 14 sts)*
Row 19: P14, turn and cast on 12 sts, turn back and p to end. *(40 sts)*
Work 6 rows in st st beg with a k row.
Row 26: Bind (cast) off 4 sts, k to end. *(36 sts)*
Row 27: Bind (cast) off 4 sts pwise, p to end. *(32 sts)*

Rep rows 26–27 once more. *(24 sts)*
Row 30: K2, ssk, k to last 4 sts, k2tog, k2. *(22 sts)*
Row 31: Purl.
Rep rows 30–31 twice more. *(18 sts)*
Knit 3 rows.
Bind (cast) off.

SLEEVE FRILL

With RS facing, pick up and knit 14 sts along wrist edge of one sleeve.
Row 2: [Inc pwise, p1] to end. *(21 sts)*
Work 5 rows in st st beg with a k row.
Bind (cast) off kwise.
Rep for other sleeve.

TO MAKE UP TOP

Join sleeve and side seams.
Weave in all loose ends.

vest (waistcoat)

FRONT

(MAKE 2)
Cast on 7 sts in D.
Purl 3 rows.
Row 4 (RS): P2, [yo, skpo] twice, p1.
Rep rows 1–4 (last 4 rows) 8 times more.
Purl 3 rows.
Break yarn and put sts on holder or spare needle.

BACK

(MAKE 1)
Cast on 15 sts.
Purl 3 rows.
Row 4 (RS): P2, [yo, skpo] to last st, p1.
Rep rows 1–4 (last 4 rows) 8 times more.
Purl 3 rows.
Break yarn and put sts on holder or spare needle.

COLLAR

With RS of each piece facing, work across one front piece, the back piece then the second front piece. *(30 sts)*
Row 1: [P2tog] to end. *(15 sts)*
Purl 2 rows.
Bind (cast) off pwise.

TO MAKE UP VEST (WAISTCOAT)
Join side seams, leaving a gap below collar to create armholes. Weave in all loose ends.

shorts

(MAKE 1)
Cast on 18 sts in E.
Work 7 rows in st st beg with a p row.
Break yarn and leave sts on needle.
Cast on 18 sts on needle without sts.
Work 7 rows in st st beg with a p row.
Now work across all 36 sts.
Work 10 rows in st st beg with a k row.
Next row: [K1, p1] to end.
Rep last row 3 times more.
Bind (cast) off keeping to the k1, p1 patt.

TO MAKE UP SHORTS
Sew inside leg and back seams. Weave in all loose ends. Roll up lower edges of legs and secure with a few stitches.

boots

(MAKE 2)
Cast on 26 sts in B.
Knit 3 rows.
Break B and join in F.
Work 4 rows in st st beg with a k row.
Row 8: K7, [ssk] 3 times, [k2tog] 3 times, k to end. (20 sts)
Row 9: Purl.
Row 10: K6, [ssk] twice, [k2tog] twice, k to end. (16 sts)
Work 6 rows in st st beg with a p row.
Row 17: Knit.
Bind (cast) off loosely.

TO MAKE UP BOOTS
Fold boot pieces in half so that the right side is on the inside and oversew sole (see page 125). Turn the pieces the right way out and sew the back seams. Using B, work a row of three straight stitches (see page 124) on front of boots to represent laces. Weave in all loose ends.

purse

BACK AND FLAP
(MAKE 1)
Cast on 5 sts in G.
Row 1: Inc, k to last 2 sts, inc, k1. (7 sts)
Row 2: Knit.
Row 3: K1, m1, k to last st, m1, k1. (9 sts)
Row 4: Knit.
Rep rows 3–4, 3 times more. (15 sts)
Knit 4 rows.
Row 15: K1, ssk, k to last 3 sts, k2tog, k1. (13 sts)
Knit 3 rows.
Row 19: K1, ssk, k to last 3 sts, k2tog, k1.* (11 sts)
Knit 5 rows.
Row 25: K1, ssk, k to last 3 sts, k2tog, k1. (9 sts)
Row 26: Knit.
Rep rows 25–26 once more. (7 sts)
Row 29: K1, ssk, k1, k2tog, k1. (5 sts)
Row 30: K2, bind (cast) off 1 st, k to end. (4 sts in 2 groups of 2 sts)
Row 31: Ssk, turn and cast on 1 st, turn back, k2tog. (3 sts)
Bind (cast) off.

FRONT
(MAKE 1)
Work as for back to *.
Bind (cast) off.

STRAP
(MAKE 1)
Using J10 (6mm) crochet hook and H trebled, work a 7-in (18-cm) crochet chain (see page 125). Trim at the end and separate yarn to form tassels.

TO MAKE UP PURSE
Join front of purse to back, leaving top flap free. Sew button and strap in place. Weave in all loose ends.

necklace

Thread the Hamsa charm onto middle of 16-in (40-cm) length of Ecru 101 yarn. Add 9 beads to each side, making a knot in the yarn between the charm and the first bead on each side and between each bead. Tie another knot after the end beads to keep all the beads in place. Make a knot at each end of the yarn before tying the necklace around the doll's neck.

hairband

Using D3 (3.25mm) crochet hook and G, work a 9-in (23-cm) crochet chain (see page 125). Tie into a bow and secure free ends to doll's hair, using photograph as a guide.

Carlos the Cat

Cheeky, sassy, and more than a little bit bossy, Carlos is kingpin cat in his neighborhood. Favorite activities include chasing mice, howling, and climbing trees. But best of all, he loves lounging around. There's no doubt about it, Carlos is one cool cat.

main doll

Work body, head, and arms in A, following pattern for Renée Rabbit, see page 60.

LEGS

(MAKE 2)
Cast on 24 sts in A.
Work 4 rows in st st beg with a k row.
Row 5: K6, [ssk] 3 times, [k2tog] 3 times, k to end. (18 sts)
Row 6: Purl.
Row 7: K5, [ssk] twice, [k2tog] twice, k to end. (14 sts)
Row 8: Purl.
Row 9: K5, ssk, k2tog, k to end. (12 sts)
Work 29 rows in st st beg with a p row.
Bind (cast) off.

EARS

(MAKE 4)
Cast on 6 sts in A.
Work 2 rows in st st beg with a k row.
Row 3: Ssk, k2, k2tog. (4 sts)
Row 4: P2tog, p2tog tbl. (2 sts)
Row 5: K2tog. (1 st)
Fasten off.

TO MAKE UP CAT

Make up main animal as for basic doll explained on page 9.

For the ears, place two pieces right sides together and oversew (see page 125) around the two sides, leaving the lower edges open. Repeat with two remaining pieces to make two ears. Turn the right way out and sew in position using the photograph as a guide.

For eyes, work French knots (see page 124) using black yarn. Using white yarn, work a circle of chain stitch (see page 124) around each French knot. Using black yarn, work a small triangle in satin stitch (see page 124) for the nose, using the photograph as a guide. Add a straight vertical stitch at the bottom. Using a single strand of black yarn, work a few whiskers. Weave in all loose ends.

top

FRONT
(MAKE 1)

Cast on 24 sts in B.

Row 1: Knit.

Work 16 rows in st st beg with a k row.

Break B and join in C.*

Work 3 rows in st st beg with a k row.

Next row: P10, k4, p to end.

Next row: Knit.

Next row: P10, k4, p to end.

Mark both ends of last row with stitch marker or small safety pin.

Next row: K2, ssk, k8, turn. *(11 sts)*

Work on 11 sts just worked, leaving rem sts on needle.

Next row: K2, p to end.

Next row: K2, ssk, k to end. *(10 sts)*

Next row: K2, p to end.

Next row: Knit.

Next row: K2, p to end.

Rep last 2 rows 3 times more.

Break yarn. Leave sts on a holder or spare needle.

Rejoin C to rem 12 sts on RS of work.

Next row: K to last 4 sts, k2tog, k2. *(11 sts)*

Next row: P to last 2 sts, k2.

Rep last 2 rows once more. *(10 sts)*

Next row: Knit.

Next row: P to last 2 sts, k2.

Rep last 2 rows 3 times more.

Break yarn. Leave these sts on a holder or spare needle.

BACK
(MAKE 1)

Work as for front to *.

Work 6 rows in st st beg with a k row.

Mark both ends of last row with stitch marker or small safety pin.

Next row: K2, ssk, k to last 4 sts, k2tog, k2. *(22 sts)*

Next row: Purl.

Rep last 2 rows once more. *(20 sts)*

Work 6 rows in st st beg with a k row.

Next row: [K2, ssk] twice, k4, [k2tog, k2] twice. *(16 sts)*

Next row: Purl.

Break yarn. Leave these sts on a holder or spare needle.

Arrange stitches so that the RS of work is facing and knit across the neck edges of the right side of the front, the back, then the left side of the front using C. *(36 sts)*

Next row: K10, [ssk] 3 times, k4, [k2tog] 3 times, k to end. *(30 sts)*

Knit 9 rows.

Bind (cast) off.

SLEEVES

With RS facing, pick up and knit 9 sts from one safety pin or marker to shoulder edges and another 9 sts from shoulder edges to second safety pin or marker. Work 18 rows in st st beg with a p row.

Bind (cast) off kwise.

Rep for second sleeve.

TO MAKE UP TOP

Join side and sleeve seams. Weave in all loose ends.

cropped pants

(MAKE 1)

Cast on 18 sts in D.

Work 26 rows in st st beg with a k row.

Break yarn and leave sts on needle.

Cast on 18 sts on needle with sts.

Row 1: Knit.

Work 26 rows in st st beg with a k row but do not break yarn.

Now work across all 36 sts.

Work 14 rows in st st beg with a k row.

Next row: [K1, p1] to end.

Rep last row once more.

Bind (cast) off keeping to the k1, p1 patt.

TO MAKE UP PANTS

Sew inside leg and back seams.

Weave in all loose ends.

Skiing Steffi

Steffi loves to get up early and head for the ski slopes, and she loves the après ski hot chocolate and cake even more. In her trendy boots, her sweater with a cool snowflake motif—and don't forget the bobble hat—Steffi cuts a dash on the slopes, and in the fashion stakes, too.

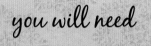

you will need

YARN AND MATERIALS
Debbie Bliss Baby Cashmerino (55% wool, 33% acrylic, 12% cashmere), 137yd (125m) per 1¾oz (50g) ball of sport weight (light DK) yarn
  ¾ ball Mink 64 (A)—head and body, arms, legs
  ¼ ball Chocolate 11 (B)—hair
  ½ ball Baby Blue 204 (C)—sweater
  Small amount of Denim 27 (D)—sweater
  ¼ ball Flame 306 (E)—pants, pom-pom for hat
  ¼ ball Citrus 18 (F)—hat
  ¼ ball Silver 12 (G)—boots
  Very small amount of Black 300 (H)—eyes

Very small amount of coral, red, or pink embroidery floss (thread) or yarn—mouth

4 x ⁵⁄₁₆in (8mm) pale gray buttons

1oz (30g) polyester toy filling

NEEDLES AND EQUIPMENT
US3 (3.25mm) knitting needles

Yarn sewing needle

Large-eyed embroidery needle

4 stitch markers or small safety pins

Pins

Coloring pencil in deep pink or red

GAUGE (TENSION)
Approximately 25 stitches and 34 rows to 4in (10cm) over st st (see also page 114)

ABBREVIATIONS
See page 127

main doll

Work as for basic pattern on page 9. Work head and body pieces, arms and legs in A.

HAIR
(MAKE 1)
Cast on 18 sts in B.
Work 4 rows in st st beg with a k row.
Row 5: Ssk, k to last 2 sts, k2tog. (16 sts)
Row 6: Purl.

Rep last 2 rows twice more. (12 sts)
Row 11: Inc, k7, turn. (9 sts)
Next row: P2tog, p to end. (8 sts)
Next row: Inc, k5, k2tog, turn.
Next row: P2tog, p to end. (7 sts)
Next row: Inc, k4, k2tog, turn.
Next row: P2tog, p to end. (6 sts)
Next row: K4, k2tog, turn. (5 sts)
Next row: P2tog, p to end. (4 sts)
Next row: K2, k2tog, turn. (3 sts)
Next row: P2tog, p1. (2 sts)
Next row: K2tog. (1 st)
Fasten off.

Rejoin yarn to rem 4 sts on RS of work.

Next row: K to last st, inc. (5 sts)
Next row: Purl.
Rep last 2 rows once more. (6 sts)
Next row: Ssk, k to last st, inc.
Next row: Purl.
Next row: Ssk, k to end. (5 sts)
Next row: P to last 2 sts, p2tog. (4 sts)
Rep last 2 rows once more. (2 sts)
Next row: K2tog. (1 st)
Fasten off.

BUNCHES

(MAKE 2)

Cast on 20 sts in B.

*Bind (cast) off 19 sts.

Transfer rem st from right-hand to left-hand needle.

Cast on 19 sts.**

Rep from * to ** once more.

Bind (cast) off.

TO MAKE UP DOLL

Make up main doll as explained on page 9.

For eyes, work French knots (see page 124) using H. Embroider mouth in straight stitch (see page 124) using embroidery floss (thread) or a separated strand of yarn. Work nose by working a couple of chain stitches (see page 124) in A, in a short vertical line. To make the nose slightly more prominent, work another couple of chain stitches over the ones you have just sewn. Add a bit of color to the cheeks using the coloring pencil. Seam the hair piece to form a cap shape. Pin then oversew (see page 125) the hair piece to head, using matching yarn. Stitch bunches in place at the side of the head, using photograph as a guide.

Weave in all loose ends.

sweater

FRONT

(MAKE 1)

Cast on 23 sts in C.

Row 1: Knit.

Row 2: Join in D and [k1 in C, k1 in D] to last st, k1 in C.

Row 3: [P1 in C, p1 in D] to last st, p1 in C.

Break D.*

Work 6 rows in st st beg with a k row.

Row 10: K11 in C, k1 in D, k in C to end.

The st worked in D on row 10 represents the lowest point of the Fair Isle star (see chart, below). Follow chart patt while working as folls:

Work 7 rows in st st beg with a p row.

Mark beg and end of last row with a stitch marker or small safety pin.

Row 18: K1, ssk, k to last 3 sts, k2tog, k1. *(21 sts)*

Row 19: Purl.

Rep rows 18–19 once more. *(19 sts)*

Row 22: Knit.

Break D (Fair Isle star now complete).

Work 5 rows in st st beg with a p row.

Row 28: Bind (cast) off 3 sts, k to end. *(16 sts)*

Row 29: Bind (cast) off 3 sts pwise, p to end. *(13 sts)*

Work 4 rows in st st beg with a k row.

Bind (cast) off loosely.

BACK

(MAKE 1)

Work as for front to *.

Work 14 rows in st st beg with a k row.

Mark beg and end of last row with stitch marker or small safety pin.

Row 18: K1, ssk, k to last 3 sts, k2tog, k1. *(21 sts)*

Row 19: Purl.

Rep rows 18–19 once more. *(19 sts)*

Work 6 rows in st st beg with a k row.

Row 28: Bind (cast) off 3 sts, k to end. *(16 sts)*

Row 29: Bind (cast) off 3 sts pwise, p to end. *(13 sts)*

Work 4 rows in st st beg with a k row.

Bind (cast) off loosely.

SLEEVES

(MAKE 2)

Cast on 17 sts in C.

Row 1: Knit.

Row 2: Join in D and [k1 in C, k1 in D] to last st, k1 in C.

Row 3: [P1 in C, p1 in D] to last st, p1 in C.

Break D and work rem of sleeve in C.

Work 20 rows in st st.

Bind (cast) off.

Sew side seams from lower edge to stitch markers and sew roll-neck and shoulder seams, remembering that roll-neck will roll down and the "wrong" side of your work will be visible. Sew sleeve seams. Insert sleeves into armholes and sew in place from the inside. Weave in all loose ends.

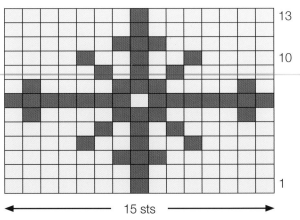

☐ Baby Blue 204
■ Denim 27

15 sts

pants

(MAKE 1)
Cast on 18 sts in E.
Row 1: Knit.
Work 26 rows in st st beg with a
k row.
Break yarn and leave sts on needle.
Cast on 18 sts on empty needle.
Row 1: Knit.
Work 26 rows in st st beg with a k row
but do not break yarn.
Now work across all 36 sts.
Work 11 rows in st st beg with a
k row.
Next row: [K1, p1] to end.
Rep last row once more.
Bind (cast) off keeping to the k1,
p1 patt.

TO MAKE UP PANTS
Sew inside leg and back seams.
Weave in all loose ends.

hat

(MAKE 1)
Cast on 36 sts in F.
Row 1: [K1, p1] to end.
Rep row 1 once more.
Row 3: K4, [m1, k4] to end. *(44 sts)*
Work 13 rows in st st beg with a
p row.
Row 17: [K2tog] to end. *(22 sts)*
Row 18: Purl.
Row 19: [K2tog] to end. *(11 sts)*
Row 20: P1, [p2tog] to end. *(6 sts)*
Break yarn, thread through rem sts,
and secure.

POM-POM
(MAKE 1)
Wrap a length of E around two fingers
approx. 20 times. Slip yarn off fingers
and tie in the middle. Trim edges then
shape into a small pom-pom approx.
1¼in (3cm) in diameter.

TO MAKE UP HAT
Sew back seam of hat and sew
pom-pom in place. Weave in all
loose ends.

boots

FOOT
(MAKE 2)
Cast on 26 sts in G.
Row 1: Knit.
Row 2: Purl.
Row 3: Knit.
Rep rows 1–3 once more.
Row 7: Purl.
Row 8: K7, [ssk] 3 times, [k2tog]
3 times, k to end. *(20 sts)*
Row 9: Purl.
Row 10: K6, [ssk] twice, [k2tog] twice,
k to end. *(16 sts)*
Work 2 rows in st st beg with a p row.
Bind (cast) off.

UPPER
(MAKE 2)
Cast on 11 sts in G.
Row 1: K1, [p1, k1] to end.
Row 2: P1, [k1, p1] to end.
Rep rows 1–2, 12 times more.
Bind (cast) off, keeping to the k1,
p1 patt.

TO MAKE UP BOOTS
Fold foot part of boot pieces in half so
that the right side is on the inside and
oversew (see page 125) sole. Turn the
pieces the right way out and sew the
back seams. Shape the upper parts of
the boot into circles. The short sides of
the piece should overlap slightly, with
the cast-on edge on the outside.
Stitch cast-on edge in place. Stitch
uppers to foot parts of boot. The
overlapped edges should face
backward and be on the outside
edge of both boots. Using a
separated strand of D, sew buttons
in place on boot uppers, using
photograph as a guide.

Penelope the Pop Star

Penelope loves strutting across stages all over the world, bringing her own brand of music to her adoring fans. In the world of pop stardom, you can do your own thing, whether it's pink hair, an orange mini skirt, or long green boots. And don't forget the jewel in her belly button!

you will need

YARN AND MATERIALS

Debbie Bliss Baby Cashmerino (55% wool, 33% acrylic, 12% cashmere), 137yd (125m) per 1¾oz (50g) ball of sport weight (light DK) yarn
- ½ ball Clotted Cream 65 (A)—head and body, arms
- ¼ ball Citrus 18 (B)—legs
- ¼ ball Lipstick Pink 78 (C)—hair, bootlaces, sewing on jacket buttons
- Small amount Acid Yellow 91 (D)—crop top
- ½ ball Mist 57 (E)—jacket
- ¼ ball Orange 92 (F)—skirt
- Small amount of Sapphire 89 (G)—eyeshadow and underpants
- ¼ ball Leaf 90 (H)—boots
- Very small amount of Black 300 (J)—eyes

Very small amount of coral, red, or pink embroidery floss (thread) or yarn—mouth

2 x ¾in (2cm) chrome curtain rings

7-in (18-cm) length of narrow green ribbon

Silver star charm and a short length of metallic yarn or embroidery floss (thread)

Sew-on blue gem for belly button

⅜in (10mm) green button

2 x ⁵⁄₁₆in (8mm) mid-gray buttons

1oz (30g) polyester toy filling

NEEDLES AND EQUIPMENT

US3 (3.25mm) knitting needles

D3 (3.25mm) crochet hook (or one of similar size)

Yarn sewing needle

Large-eyed embroidery needle

Pins

Coloring pencil in deep pink or red

GAUGE (TENSION)

Approximately 25 stitches and 34 rows to 4in (10cm) over st st (see also page 114)

ABBREVIATIONS

See page 127

main doll

Work as for basic pattern on page 9.
Work head and body pieces and arms and in A.
Work legs in B.

HAIR

(MAKE 1)
Cast on 18 sts in C.
Work 4 rows in st st beg with a k row.
Row 5: Ssk, k to last 2 sts, k2tog. *(16 sts)*
Row 6: Purl.
Rep last 2 rows twice more. *(12 sts)*
Row 11: Inc, k to last 2 sts, inc, k1. *(14 sts)*
Row 12: Purl.
Row 13: Inc, k4, k2tog, turn and work on 7 sts just worked, leaving rem sts on needle.
Next row: P2tog, p to end. *(6 sts)*
Next row: Inc, k3, k2tog.
Next row: P2tog, p to end. *(5 sts)*
Next row: K3, k2tog. *(4 sts)*
Next row: P2tog, p2. *(3 sts)*
Next row: K1, k2tog. *(2 sts)*
Next row: P2tog. *(1 st)*
Fasten off.
Rejoin yarn to rem 7 sts on RS of work.
Next row: Ssk, k3, inc, k1.
Next row: P to last 2 sts, p2tog tbl. *(6 sts)*
Next row: Ssk, k2, inc, k1.

Next row: P to last 2 sts, p2tog tbl. *(5 sts)*
Next row: Ssk, k to end. *(4 sts)*
Next row: P2, p2tog tbl. *(3 sts)*
Next row: Ssk, k1. *(2 sts)*
Next row: P2tog. *(1 st)*
Fasten off.

BUN
(MAKE 1)
Cast on 5 sts in C.
Row 1: [Inc] 5 times. *(10 sts)*
Row 2: Purl.
Row 3: [Inc] 10 times. *(20 sts)*
Work 3 rows in st st beg with a p row.
Row 7: [K2tog] 10 times. *(10 sts)*
Row 8: Purl.
Row 9: [K2tog] 5 times. *(5 sts)*
Break yarn and thread through rem sts.

TO MAKE UP DOLL
Make up main doll as explained on page 9.
For eyes, work French knots (see page 124) using yarn J. For the eyeshadow, work a short, curved row of chain stitch just above the eye (see page 124), using G. Embroider mouth in straight stitch (see page 124) using

embroidery floss (thread) or a separated strand of yarn. Work nose by working a couple of chain stitches in A, in a short vertical line. To make the nose slightly more prominent, work another couple of chain stitches over the ones you have just sewn. For the ears, work a few chain stitches in A, in a short vertical line at the side of the head, in line with the eyes. Then work another row of chain stitches on top to make the ears a bit more prominent. Add a bit of color to the cheeks using the coloring pencil.
Sew curtain rings on for earrings, using the photograph as a guide. Thread star charm onto metallic embroidery floss (thread) and tie round doll's neck.
Fasten sew-on gem to belly.
Seam the hair piece to form a cap shape. Pin then oversew (see page 125) the hair piece to head, using matching yarn. For bun, run yarn tail around the outside of the knitted piece, very close to the edge. Pull up into a small sphere shape, stuffing with a small piece of stuffing as you go. Stitch in place on top of the head. Tie ribbon around base of bun.
Weave in all loose ends.

crop top

The top is knitted from the top down.
(MAKE 1)
Cast on 24 sts in D.
Row 1: Knit.
Row 2: K6, m1, k1, m1, k10, m1, k1, m1, k to end. *(28 sts)*
Row 3: K2, p to last 2 sts, k2.
Row 4: K6, m1, k3, m1, k10, m1, k3, m1, k to end. *(32 sts)*
Row 5: K2, p to last 2 sts, k2.
Row 6: K6, m1, k5, m1, k10, m1, k5, m1, k to end. *(36 sts)*
Row 7: K2, p to last 2 sts, k2.
Row 8: K6, m1, k7, m1, k10, m1, k7, m1, k to end. *(40 sts)*
Row 9: K2, p5, bind (cast) off 7 sts kwise, (1 st rem on needle from binding/casting off), p11, bind (cast) off 7 sts kwise, (1 st rem on needle from binding/casting off), p4, k2. *(26 sts)*

Row 10: K7, turn, cast on 3 sts, turn, k12, turn, cast on 3 sts, turn, k to end. *(32 sts)*
Row 11: K2, p to last 2 sts, k2.
Knit 2 rows.
Row 14: K1, [yo, k2tog] to last st, k1.
Row 15: Knit.
Bind (cast) off pwise.

TO MAKE UP TOP
Sew the back seam of the top, from the lower edge up to the base of the back opening worked in garter stitch. Using a yarn tail at the top of the back of the top, use the crochet hook to work a few crochet chains (see page 125). Secure the free end of the chain to form a button loop. Sew green button to corresponding side. Weave in all loose ends.

jacket

BACK AND FRONT
(MAKE 1)
Cast on 44 sts in E.
Knit 4 rows.
Row 5: Knit.
Row 6: K3, p to last 3 sts, k3.
Rep rows 5–6, 3 times more.
Row 13: K11, turn.
Work on these 11 sts only, leaving rem sts on needle.
Next row: P to last 3 sts, k3.
Next row: Knit.
Next row: P to last 3 sts, k3.
Next row: Knit.
Break yarn and rejoin it to rem 33 sts on RS of work.
Next row: K22, turn.
Work on these 22 sts only, leaving rem sts on needle.
Work 5 rows in st st beg with a p row.
Next row: K1, ssk, k to last 3 sts, k2tog, k1. *(20 sts)*
Next row: Purl.
Next row: K1, ssk, k to last 3 sts, k2tog, k1. *(18 sts)*
Break yarn and rejoin it to rem 11 sts on RS of work.
Next row: Knit.
Next row: K3, p to end.
Rep last 2 rows 3 times more.
Next row: Knit.
Now work across all 40 sts.

Next row: K3, p to last 3 sts, k3.
Next row: Bind (cast) off 3 sts pwise,
(1 st rem on needle from binding/
casting off), k5, ssk, k2tog, k2, ssk,
k6, k2tog, k2, ssk, k2tog, k to end.
(31 sts)
Next row: Bind (cast) off 3 sts, p to
last 2 sts, k2. *(28 sts)*
Knit 5 rows.
Bind (cast) off.

SLEEVES
(MAKE 2)
Cast on 16 sts in E.
Knit 4 rows.
Work 18 rows in st st beg with a
k row.
Bind (cast) off.

TO MAKE UP JACKET
Sew sleeve seams. Insert into
armholes and stitch in place from the
inside. Sew gray buttons onto jacket
using separated strand of C. The gaps
between the knitted stitches can be
used for buttonholes. Weave in all
loose ends.

skirt

(MAKE 1)
Cast on 52 sts in F.
Row 1: [K1, yo, k2tog] to last st, k1.
Row 2: P1, [p1, k1, p1] to end.
Row 3: [K1, k2tog, yo] to last st, k1.

Row 4: P1, [k1, p2] to end.
Rep rows 1–4 twice more.
Rep rows 1–2 once more.
Row 15: K1, [k2tog, k1] to end.
(35 sts)
Row 16: [K3, k2tog] twice, k4, k2tog,
k3, k2tog, k4, [k2tog, k3] twice.
(29 sts)
Knit 2 rows.
Bind (cast) off.

TO MAKE UP SKIRT
Join back seam. Weave in all
loose ends.

underpants

(MAKE 1)
Cast on 16 sts in G.
Knit 2 rows.
Break yarn and cast on another 16 sts
on the same needle.
Knit 2 rows.
Now work across all 32 sts.
Work 8 rows in st st beg with a k row.
Next row: [K1, p1] to end.
Rep last row once more.
Bind (cast) off keeping to the k1,
p1 patt.

TO MAKE UP UNDERPANTS
Join inside leg and back seams.
Weave in all loose ends.

boots

(MAKE 2)
Cast on 26 sts in H.
Work 4 rows in st st beg with a k row.
Row 5: K7, [ssk] 3 times, [k2tog]
3 times, k to end. *(20 sts)*
Row 6: Purl.
Row 7: K6, [ssk] twice, [k2tog] twice,
k to end. *(16 sts)*
Work 16 rows in st st beg with a
p row.
Row 24: Knit.
Bind (cast) off.

TO MAKE UP BOOTS
Fold boot pieces in half so that
the right side is on the inside and
oversew sole. Turn the pieces the right
way out and sew the back seams.
Using C, work three cross stitches on
the boot, using the photograph as a
guide, to represent laces. Weave in all
loose ends.

Surfer Dude Ben

From his tousled blond curls to his pool slides, Ben is a Californian surfing superstar. Board shorts and a shirt make a simple outfit, and his beads are a suitably cool finishing touch.

you will need

YARN AND MATERIALS

FOR DOLL

Debbie Bliss Baby Cashmerino (55% wool, 33% acrylic, 12% cashmere), 137yd (125m) per 1¾oz (50g) ball of sport weight (light DK) yarn
- ¾ ball of Clotted Cream 65 (A)—head and body, arms, legs
- Small amount of Chocolate 11 (B)—pool slide shoes
- ¼ ball of Primrose 01 (C)—hair
- ¼ ball of Coral 86 (D)—shirt
- ¼ ball of Drake 302 (E)—shorts
- Small amount of White 100 (F)— decoration on shorts
- Very small amount of Black 300 (G)—eyes

Very small amount of coral, red, or pink embroidery floss (thread) or yarn—mouth

3 x small colored beads, some thin black waxed cord, and some colored embroidery floss (thread) for jewelry

1oz (30g) polyester toy filling

FOR SURFBOARD

Debbie Bliss Baby Cashmerino (55% wool, 33% acrylic, 12% cashmere), 137yd (125m) per 1¾oz (50g) ball of sport weight (light DK) yarn
- ¼ ball of Sapphire 89 (H)
- ½ ball of White 100 (J)
- Small amount of Pool 71 (L)

4 x 10in (10 x 25cm) piece of thick acetate

NEEDLES AND EQUIPMENT

US3 (3.25mm) knitting needles

D3 (3.25mm) crochet hook (or one of similar size)

Yarn sewing needle

Large-eyed embroidery needle

Coloring pencil in deep pink or red (optional)

GAUGE (TENSION)

Approximately 25 stitches and 34 rows to 4in (10cm) over st st (see also page 114)

ABBREVIATIONS

See page 127

main doll

Work as for basic pattern on page 9. Work head and body piece and arms in A.

LEGS

(MAKE 2)
Cast on 24 sts in B.
Knit 2 rows.
Break B and join in A.
Work 2 rows in st st beg with a k row.
Row 5: K6, [ssk] 3 times, [k2tog] 3 times, k to end. *(18 sts)*
Row 6: Purl.

Row 7: K5, [ssk] twice, [k2tog] twice, k to end. *(14 sts)*
Row 8: Purl.
Row 9: K5, ssk, k2tog, k to end. *(12 sts)*
Work 29 rows in st st beg with a p row.
Bind (cast) off.

HAIR
(MAKE 1)
Cast on 20 sts in C.
Bind (cast) off 19 sts and transfer rem st from right-hand to left-hand needle. Cast on 19 sts. (20 sts)
Rep from * to * 10 times.
Bind (cast) off 19 sts. (1 st)
Row 1: Pick up and k 35 sts across top of fringe. (36 sts)
Work 3 rows in st st beg with a p row.
Row 5: K7, ssk, k2tog, k14, ssk, k2tog, k to end. (32 sts)
Row 6: Purl.
Row 7: K6, ssk, k2tog, k12, ssk, k2tog, k to end. (28 sts)
Row 8: Purl.
Row 9: K5, ssk, k2tog, k10, ssk, k2tog, k to end. (24 sts)
Bind (cast) off.

TO MAKE UP DOLL
Make up main doll as explained on page 9. For eyes, work French knots (see page 124) using black yarn. Embroider mouth by working two straight stitches (see page 124) in embroidery floss (thread). Work nose by working a few chain stitches (see page 124) in A, in a short vertical line. To make the nose slightly more prominent, work another few chain stitches over the ones you have just sewn. Add a bit of color to the cheeks using the coloring pencil. Seam the hair piece to form a cap shape. Pin then oversew (see page 125) the hair piece to head, using matching yarn. For the ears, work a few chain stitches in A in a short

vertical line at the side of the head, in line with the eyes. Then work another row of chain stitches on top to make the ears a bit more prominent. Thread three beads onto a short length of the black cord, knot either side of beads, and tie around neck for necklace. For black bracelet, braid (plait) three lengths of black cord and tie round wrist. For colored bracelets, braid (plait) three lengths of embroidery floss (thread) and tie around wrist.
For each shoe strap, cast on 6 sts in B. Bind (cast) off. Sew across top of each foot.

shirt

FRONT AND BACK
(MAKE 1)
Cast on 36 sts in D.
Knit 2 rows.
Row 3: K2, p to last 2 sts, k2.
Row 4: Knit.
Row 5: K2, p to last 2 sts, k2.
Rep rows 4–5, 4 times more.
Row 14: K9, turn.
Work on these 9 sts only, leaving rem sts on needle.
Next row: P to last 2 sts, k2.
Next row: Knit.
Next row: P to last 2 sts, k2.
Rep last 2 rows once more.
Next row: Knit.
Break yarn and rejoin it to rem sts on RS of work.
Next row: K18, turn.
Work on these 18 sts only, leaving rem sts on needle.
Work 6 rows in st st beg with a p row.
Break yarn and rejoin it to rem 9 sts on RS of work.
Next row: Knit.
Next row: K2, p to end.
Rep last 2 rows twice more.
Next row: Knit.
Now work across all 36 sts.
Next row: K2, p to last 2 sts, k2.
Next row: K5, [ssk] twice, [k2tog] twice, k10, [ssk] twice, [k2tog] twice, k to end. (28 sts)
Knit 6 rows.
Bind (cast) off.

SLEEVES
(MAKE 2)
Cast on 14 sts in D.
Knit 2 rows.
Work 7 rows in st st beg with a p row.
Bind (cast) off.

TO MAKE UP SHIRT
Sew sleeve seams using mattress stitch (see page 126). Insert sleeves into shirt and oversew (see page 125) around armholes from the inside. Weave in all loose ends.

shorts
(MAKE 1)
Cast on 18 sts in E.
Work 3 rows in st st beg with a p row.
Leave E at side and join in F.
Work 2 rows in st st beg with a k row.
Leave F at side and cont in E.
Work 2 rows in st st beg with a k row.
Leave E at side and cont in F.
Work 2 rows in st st beg with a k row.
Break F and cont in E.
Work 4 rows in st st beg with a k row.
Break yarn and leave sts on needle.
Cast on 18 sts in E on needle without sts.
Work 13 rows in st st beg with a p row.
Now work across all 36 sts.
Work 11 rows in st st beg with a k row.
Break E and work rem of piece in F.
Next row: Purl.
Next row: [K1, p1] to end.
Rep last row once more.
Bind (cast) off keeping to k1, p1 patt.

TO MAKE UP SHORTS
Sew inside leg and back seam using mattress stitch (see page 126). Embroider a flower shape using a separated strand of J and a small chain stitch (see page 124) on the shorts, as shown in the photo. Weave in all loose ends.

surfboard

TOP
(MAKE 1)
Cast on 12 sts in H.
Work 6 rows in st st beg with a k row.
Row 7: K1, m1, k to last st, m1, k1. (14 sts)
Work 7 rows in st st beg with a p row.
Row 15: K1, m1, k to last st, m1, k1. (16 sts)
Work 7 rows in st st beg with a p row.
Row 23: K1, m1, k to last st, m1, k1. (18 sts)

Row 24: Purl.
Row 25: K to last 2 sts, join in J and k2.
Row 26: P3 in J, p in H to end.
Row 27: K in H to last 4 sts, k in J to end.
Row 28: P5 in J, p in H to end.
Row 29: K in H to last 6 sts, k in J to end.
Row 30: P7 in J, p in H to end.
Row 31: K1, m1, k9 in H, k in J to last st, m1, k1. *(20 sts)*
Row 32: P10 in J, p in H to end.
Row 33: K9 in H, k in J to end.
Row 34: P12 in J, p in H to end.
Row 35: K7 in H, k in J to end.
Row 36: P14 in J, p in H to end.
Row 37: K5 in H, k in J to end.
Row 38: P16 in J, p in H to end.
Row 39: K3 in H, k in J to end.
Row 40: P in J to last 2 sts, p in H to end.
Break H and cont in J.
Work 8 rows in st st beg with a k row.
Row 49: K in J to last 2 sts, join in L and k to end.
Row 50: P3 in L, p in J to end.
Row 51: K16 in J, k in L to end.
Row 52: P5 in L, p in J to end.
Row 53: K1, ssk, k11 in J, k3, k2tog, k1 in L. *(18 sts)*
Row 54: P6 in L, p in J to end.
Row 55: K11 in J, k in L to end.
Row 56: P8 in L, p in J to end.
Row 57: K9 in J, k in L to end.
Row 58: P10 in L, p in J to end.
Row 59: K1, ssk, k4 in J; k8, k2tog, k1 in L. *(16 sts)*
Row 60: P11 in L, p in J to end.
Row 61: K4 in J, k in L to end.
Row 62: P13 in L, p in J to end.
Row 63: K1, ssk in J; k in L to last 3 sts, k2tog, k1. *(14 sts)*
Break J and work rest of surfboard top in L only.
Work 3 rows in st st beg with a p row.
Row 67: K1, ssk, k to last 3 sts, k2tog, k1. *(12 sts)*
Row 68: Purl.
Row 69: K1, ssk, k to last 3 sts, k2tog, k1. *(10 sts)*
Bind (cast) off pwise.

BASE
(MAKE 1)
Cast on 12 sts in J.
Work 6 rows in st st beg with a k row.
Row 7: K1, m1, k to last st, m1, k1. *(14 sts)*
Work 7 rows in st st beg with a p row.
Rep rows 7–14 (last 8 rows) twice more. *(18 sts)*

Row 31: K1, m1, k to last st, m1, k1. *(20 sts)*
Work 21 rows in st st beg with a p row.
Row 53: K1, ssk, k to last 3 sts, k2tog, k1. *(18 sts)*
Work 5 rows in st st beg with a p row.
Row 59: K1, ssk, k to last 3 sts, k2tog, k1. *(16 sts)*
Work 3 rows in st st beg with a p row.
Rep rows 59–62 (last 4 rows) once more. *(14 sts)*
Row 67: K1, ssk, k to last 3 sts, k2tog, k1. *(12 sts)*
Row 68: Purl.
Row 69: K1, ssk, k to last 3 sts, k2tog, k1. *(10 sts)*
Bind (cast) off pwise.

TO MAKE UP SURFBOARD
Weave in all loose ends. Cut the surfboard shape from thick acetate (we used the cover of an old plastic ring binder), using the template on the right. Join the top and base together using mattress stitch (see page 126), leaving the lower edge open. Stretch the knitted piece and insert the surfboard shape. Close the gap using mattress stitch.

SURFBOARD TEMPLATE
full size

Laura the Land Girl

Laura's job is to till the soil and grow vegetables, so it's just as well she loves the open air, whatever the weather. She needs practical clothes, so these dungarees fit the bill perfectly. And I've added a retro-style top and hairband, just to complete the land girl look.

you will need

YARN AND MATERIALS

Debbie Bliss Baby Cashmerino (55% wool, 33% acrylic, 12% cashmere), 137yd (125m) per 1¾oz (50g) ball of sport weight (light DK) yarn
- ¾ ball Clotted Cream 65 (A)—head and body, arms, legs
- ¼ ball Sienna 67 (B)—hair
- ¼ ball Bamboo 307 (C)—T-shirt
- Small amount of Pool 71 (D)—dungarees
- ½ ball Royal 70 (E)—dungarees
- Small amount of Mink 64 (F)—shoes, belt
- Small amount of Drake 302 (G)—hairband
- Very small amount of Black 300 (H)—eyes, belt buckle, shoe laces

Very small amount of coral, red, or pink embroidery floss (thread) or yarn—mouth

1oz (30g) polyester toy filling

NEEDLES AND EQUIPMENT

US3 (3.25mm) knitting needles

Yarn sewing needle

Large-eyed embroidery needle

4 stitch markers or small safety pins

Pins

Coloring pencil in deep pink or red (optional)

GAUGE (TENSION)

Approximately 25 stitches and 34 rows to 4in (10cm) over st st (see also page 114)

ABBREVIATIONS

See page 127

main doll

Work as for basic pattern on page 9. Work head and body pieces, arms and legs in A.

HAIR

(MAKE 1)
Cast on 19 sts in B.
Work 6 rows in st st beg with a k row.
Cast on 15 sts, bind (cast) off 18 sts.
*Transfer rem st from right-hand to left-hand needle.
Cast on 15 sts, bind (cast) off 18 sts.**
Rep from * to ** 4 times.
Transfer rem st from right-hand to left-hand needle.
Cast on 15 sts, bind (cast) off.
With RS facing, pick up and k 19 sts along long side of main hair piece and work a corresponding fringe along this side.
Cast on 15 sts.
Bind (cast) off 18 sts.
*Transfer rem st from right-hand to left-hand needle.
Cast on 15 sts, bind (cast) off 18 sts.**
Rep from * to ** 4 times.
Transfer rem st from right-hand to left-hand needle.
Cast on 15 sts, bind (cast) off.

TO MAKE UP DOLL

Make up main doll as explained on page 9.

For eyes, work French knots (see page 124) using H. Embroider mouth in straight stitch (see page 124) using embroidery floss (thread) or a separated strand of yarn. Work nose by working a couple of chain stitches (see page 124) in A, in a short vertical line. To make the nose slightly more prominent, work another couple of chain stitches over the ones you have just sewn. For the ears, work a few chain stitches in A, in a short vertical line at the side of the head, in line with the eyes. Then work another row of chain stitches on top to make the ears a bit more prominent. Add a bit of color to the cheeks using the coloring pencil.

Stretch hair piece over top seam of head from one ear to the other. Pin then stitch in place.

Weave in all loose ends.

t-shirt

FRONT
(MAKE 1)

Cast on 20 sts in C.

Row 1: [K1, p1] to end.

Rep row 1, 5 times more.

Work 8 rows in st st beg with a k row.

Mark beg and end of last row with stitch markers or small safety pins.*

Row 15: K1, ssk, k6, turn.

Work on the 8 sts just worked only, leaving rem sts on needle.

Next row: Cast on 2 sts, k2, p to end. *(10 sts)*

Next row: K1, ssk, k to end. *(9 sts)*

Next row: K2, p to end.

Next row: Knit.

Next row: K2, p to end.

Rep last 2 rows once more.

Next row: Bind (cast) off 3 sts, k to end. *(6 sts)*

Next row: P to last 2 sts, k2.

Bind (cast) off rem sts pwise.

Rejoin yarn to rem 11 sts on RS of work.

Next row: K to last 3 sts, k2tog, k1. *(10 sts)*

Next row: P to last 2 sts, k2.

Rep last 2 rows once more. *(9 sts)*

Next row: Knit.

Next row: P to last 2 sts, k2.

Rep last 2 rows once more.

Next row: Knit.

Next row: Bind (cast) off 3 sts pwise, (1 st rem on needle from binding/casting off), p3, k to end. *(6 sts)*

Bind (cast) off rem sts pwise.

BACK

Work as for front to *.

Row 15: K1, ssk, k to last 3 sts, k2tog, k1. *(18 sts)*

Row 16: Purl.

Rep rows 15–16 once more. *(16 sts)*

Work 4 rows in st st beg with a k row.

Row 23: Bind (cast) off 3 sts, k to end. *(13 sts)*

Row 24: Bind (cast) off 3 sts pwise, p to end. *(10 sts)*

Bind (cast) off pwise.

TO MAKE UP TOP AND WORK SLEEVES

Join shoulder seems. With RS facing and C, pick up and knit 7 sts from marker to shoulder seam and then from shoulder seam to second marker. Work 8 rows in st st beg with a p row. Bind (cast) off kwise. Work second sleeve in the same way. Join sleeve and side seams. Weave in all loose ends.

dungarees

(MAKE 1)
Cast on 18 sts in D.
Work 4 rows in st st beg with a k row.
Break D and join in E.
Work 24 rows in st st beg with a k row.
Break yarn and leave sts on needle.
Cast on 18 sts in D on needle with sts.
Work 4 rows in st st beg with a k row.
Break D and join in E.
Work 24 rows in st st beg with a k row but do not break yarn.
Now work across all 36 sts.
Work 13 rows in st st beg with a k row.
Knit 2 rows.
Bind (cast) off 12 sts kwise, (1 st rem on needle from binding/casting off), k11, bind (cast) off rem sts. *(12 sts)*
Rejoin yarn to rem sts on RS of work.
Next row: Knit.
Next row: K2, p to last 2 sts, k2.
Rep last 2 rows, 3 times more.
Knit 2 rows.
Next row: K1, p1, bind (cast) off 12 sts pwise, (1 st rem on needle from binding/casting off), k1. *(2 groups of 2 sts)*
Work on last 2 sts only, leaving rem sts on needle.
Knit 26 rows.
Next row: K2tog. *(1 st)*
Fasten off.
Rejoin yarn to rem 2 sts on WS of work.
Knit 26 rows.
Next row: K2tog. *(1 st)*
Fasten off.

BIB POCKET

(MAKE 1)
Cast on 5 sts in E.
Work 3 rows in st st beg with a k row.
Bind (cast) off kwise.

TO MAKE UP DUNGAREES

Sew inside leg and back seams. Sew pocket onto bib. Sew short edges of straps to back, crossing them over before fastening. Weave in all loose ends.

shoes

(MAKE 2)
Cast on 26 sts in F.
Work 4 rows in st st beg with a k row.
Row 5: K7, [ssk] 3 times, [k2tog] 3 times, k to end. *(20 sts)*
Row 6: Purl.
Row 7: K6, [ssk] twice, [k2tog] twice, k to end. *(16 sts)*
Row 8: Knit.
Bind (cast) off.

TO MAKE UP SHOES

Fold shoe pieces in half so that the right side is on the inside and oversew (see page 125) sole. Turn the pieces the right way out and sew the back seams. Using two separated strands of H, work two straight stitches (see page 124) on front of shoes to represent laces. Weave in all loose ends.

belt

Cast on 44 sts in F.
Bind (cast) off.

TO MAKE UP BELT

Join belt piece into a circle so that the short edges overlap slightly and the edge without the yarn tails is on the outside, to form the free end of the belt. Using H, work a square in chain stitch (see page 124) for the belt buckle.

hairband

Cast on 40 sts in G.
Bind (cast) off.

TO FINISH AND POSITION HAIRBAND

Join the hairband to the doll, just above the ears. Use the "slack" in the hairband to form the side bow, using the photograph as a guide.

techniques

On the following pages you'll find the basic knitting techniques that you will need for the patterns in this book.

gauge (tension)

The gauge (tension) is given as the number of stitches and rows needed to produce a 4-in (10-cm) square of knitting.

Using the recommended yarn and needles, cast on 8 stitches more than the gauge (tension) instruction asks for. Working in pattern, work 8 rows more than needed. Bind (cast) off loosely. Lay the swatch flat without stretching it. Lay a ruler across the stitches with the 2in (5cm) mark centered on the knitting, then put a pin in the knitting at the 0 and at the 4in (10cm) mark. Count the number of stitches between the pins. Repeat the process across the rows to count the number of rows to 4in (10cm).

If the number of stitches and rows you've counted is the same as the number asked for, you have the correct gauge (tension). If you do not have the same number then you will need to change your gauge (tension) by changing the size of your knitting needles. A good rule of thumb is that one

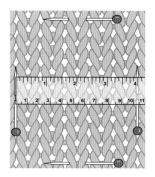

difference in needle size will create a difference of one stitch in the gauge (tension). Use larger needles to achieve fewer stitches and smaller ones to achieve more stitches.

If you are knitting the dolls in a different yarn to that suggested, you may need to knit on thinner needles than stated on the yarn's ball band to make sure the knitted fabric is dense enough for the stuffing not to show through the doll, and for the clothes to keep their shape. If your gauge (tension) is slightly different to ours, it doesn't matter. It just means your dolls and garments will be slightly larger or smaller. But it is important to knit the clothing and doll in yarns that knit to the same gauge (tension) or you'll find the clothes won't be a good fit.

holding needles

If you are a knitting novice, you will need to discover which is the most comfortable way for you to hold your needles.

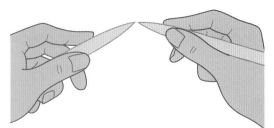

LIKE A PEN
Now try changing the right hand so you are holding the needle as you would hold a pen, with your thumb and forefinger lightly gripping the needle close to its pointed tip and the shaft resting in the crook of your thumb. As you knit, you will not need to let go of the needle but simply slide your right hand forward to manipulate the yarn.

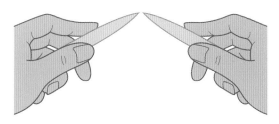

LIKE A KNIFE
Pick up the needles, one in each hand, as if you were holding a knife and fork—that is to say, with your hands lightly over the top of each needle. As you knit, you will tuck the blunt end of the right-hand needle under your arm, let go with your hand, and use your hand to manipulate the yarn, returning your hand to the needle to move the stitches along.

> ***CHOOSING NEEDLES***
> *Use short knitting needles, they're more user friendly than longer ones when you're knitting small items. Needles that are 6 or 8in (15 or 20cm) long are ideal and available from knitting shops and online stores.*

holding yarn

As you knit, you work stitches off the left-hand needle onto the right-hand needle, and the yarn needs to be held and tensioned to produce even fabric. Use either your right or left hand, depending on the method you use to make stitches.

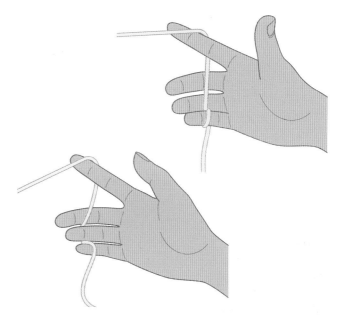

YARN IN RIGHT HAND

To knit and purl in the US/UK style (see pages 117 and 118), hold the yarn in your right hand. You can wind the yarn around your fingers in different ways, depending on how tightly you need to hold it to achieve an even gauge (tension). Try both ways shown to find out which works best for you.

To hold the yarn tightly (top right), wind it right around your little finger, under your ring and middle fingers, then pass it over your index finger, which will manipulate the yarn.

For a looser hold (below right), catch the yarn between your little and ring fingers, pass it under your middle finger, then over your index finger.

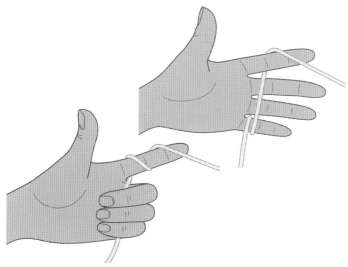

YARN IN LEFT HAND

To knit and purl in the Continental style (see pages 117 and 118), hold the yarn in your left hand. This method is sometimes easier for left-handed people to use, though many left-handers are quite comfortable knitting with the yarn in their right hand. Try the ways shown to find out which works best for you.

To hold the yarn tightly (top left), wind it right around your little finger, under your ring and middle fingers, then pass it over your index finger, which will manipulate the yarn.

For a looser hold (below left), fold your little, ring, and middle fingers over the yarn, and wind it twice around your index finger.

CHOOSING YARN

I have used Debbie Bliss Baby Cashmerino (see Suppliers, page 127) throughout this book, because it's good quality and comes in a wide range of colors. If you want to use something different, the following yarns are similar in content, gauge (tension), and general feel:
Online—Line 5 Corafino
DMC—Woolly
Millamia—Naturally Soft merino
Rooster—Baby Rooster or Almerino Baby
Sugar Bush Yarns—Bliss
Austermann—Merino 160
Spacecadet Yarn—Lyra
Unitas—Ana

Alchemy Yarns—Temple
Cloudborn Fibers—Merino Alpaca Sport
Linie—155 Supercool
Mrs Moon—Swaddle
Katia—Merino Fine
For details and more options, check out yarnsub.com. Whichever yarn you choose, please avoid budget acrylic yarns, 100% cotton, bamboo, or linen yarns: these do not have the right qualities for the patterns in this book.

For the smaller quantities given in the materials list for each doll, use the following rule of thumb:
A small amount = less than 5yd (5m)
A very small amount = less than 20in (50cm)

making a slip knot

You will need to make a slip knot to form your first cast-on stitch.

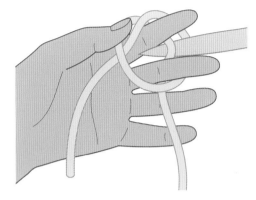 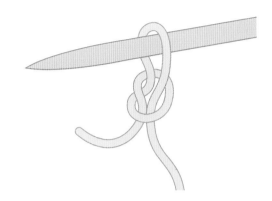

1 With the ball of yarn on your right, lay the end of the yarn on the palm of your left hand and hold it in place with your left thumb. With your right hand, take the yarn around your top two fingers to form a loop. Take the knitting needle through the back of the loop from right to left and use it to pick up the strand nearest to the yarn ball, as shown in the diagram. Pull the strand through to form a loop at the front.

2 Slip the yarn off your fingers, leaving the loop on the needle. Gently pull on both yarn ends to tighten the knot. Then pull on the yarn leading to the ball of yarn to tighten the knot on the needle.

casting on (cable method)

There are a few methods of casting on but the one used for the projects in this book is the cable method, which uses two needles.

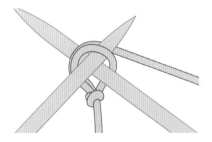  

1 Make a slip knot as shown above. Put the needle with the slip knot into your left hand. Insert the point of the other needle into the front of the slip knot and under the left-hand needle. Wind the yarn from the ball of yarn around the tip of the right-hand needle.

2 Using the tip of the needle, draw the yarn through the slip knot to form a loop. This loop is the new stitch. Slip the loop from the right-hand needle onto the left-hand needle.

3 To make the next stitch, insert the tip of the right-hand needle between the two stitches. Wind the yarn over the right-hand needle, from left to right, then draw the yarn through to form a loop. Transfer this loop to the left-hand needle. Repeat until you have cast on the right number of stitches for the project.

knit stitch

There are only two stitches to master in knitting; knit stitch and purl stitch. Most people in the English-speaking world knit using a method called English (or American) knitting. However, in parts of Europe, people prefer a method known as Continental knitting.

US/UK STYLE

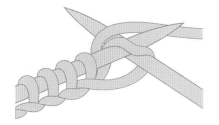  

1 Hold the needle with the cast-on stitches in your left hand, and then insert the point of the right-hand needle into the front of the first stitch from left to right. Wind the yarn around the point of the right-hand needle, from left to right.

2 With the tip of the right-hand needle, pull the yarn through the stitch to form a loop. This loop is the new stitch.

3 Slip the original stitch off the left-hand needle by gently pulling the right-hand needle to the right. Repeat these steps till you have knitted all the stitches on the left-hand needle. To work the next row, transfer the needle with all the stitches into your left hand.

CONTINENTAL STYLE

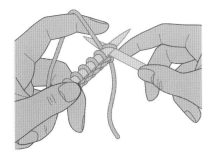 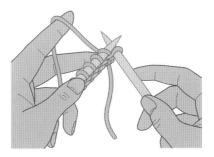 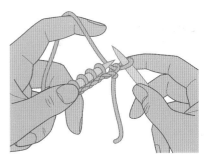

1 Hold the needle with the stitches to be knitted in your left hand, and then insert the tip of the right-hand needle into the front of the first stitch from left to right. Holding the yarn fairly taut with your left hand at the back of your work, use the tip of the right-hand needle to pick up a loop of yarn.

2 With the tip of the right-hand needle, bring the yarn through the original stitch to form a loop. This loop is the new stitch.

3 Slip the original stitch off the left-hand needle by gently pulling the right-hand needle to the right. Repeat these steps till you have knitted all the stitches on the left-hand needle. To work the next row, transfer the needle with all the stitches into your left hand.

purl stitch

As with knit stitch, purl stitch can be formed in two ways. If you are new to knitting, try both techniques to see which works better for you: left-handed people may find the Continental method easier to master.

US/UK STYLE

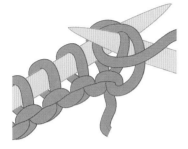  

1 Hold the needle with the stitches in your left hand, and then insert the point of the right-hand needle into the front of the first stitch from right to left. Wind the yarn around the point of the right-hand needle, from right to left.

2 With the tip of the right-hand needle, pull the yarn through the stitch to form a loop. This loop is the new stitch.

3 Slip the original stitch off the left-hand needle by gently pulling the right-hand needle to the right. Repeat these steps till you have purled all the stitches on the left-hand needle. To work the next row, transfer the needle with all the stitches into your left hand.

CONTINENTAL STYLE

1 Hold the needle with the stitches to be knitted in your left hand, and then insert the tip of the right-hand needle into the front of the first stitch from right to left. Holding the yarn fairly taut at the front of the work, move the tip of the right-hand needle under the working yarn, then push your left index finger downward, as shown, to hold the yarn around the needle.

2 With the tip of the right-hand needle, bring the yarn through the original stitch to form a loop.

3 Slip the original stitch off the left-hand needle by gently pulling the right-hand needle to the right. Repeat these steps till you have purled all the stitches on the left-hand needle. To work the next row, transfer the needle with all the stitches into your left hand.

binding (casting) off

You need to bind (cast) off the stitches to complete the projects and stop the knitting unraveling.

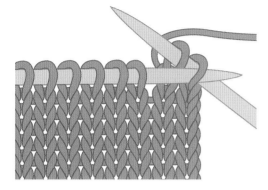

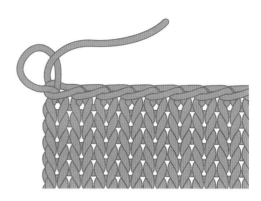

1 First knit two stitches in the normal way. With the point of the left-hand needle, pick up the first stitch you have just knitted and lift it over the second stitch. Knit another stitch so that there are two stitches on the right-hand needle again. Repeat the process of lifting the first stitch over the second stitch. Continue this process until there is just one stitch remaining on the right-hand needle.

2 Break the yarn, leaving a tail of yarn long enough to sew the work together (see page 125). Pull the tail all the way through the last stitch. Slip the stitch off the needle and pull it fairly tightly to make sure it is secure.

picking up stitches

For some projects, you will need to pick up stitches along either a horizontal edge (the cast-on or bound-/cast-off edge of your knitting), or a vertical edge (the edges of your rows of knitting).

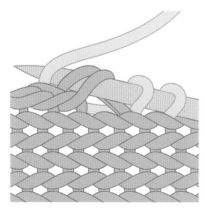

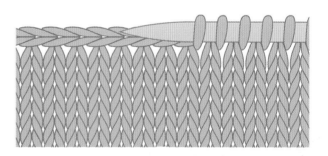

ALONG A ROW-END EDGE
With the right side of the knitting facing you, insert a knitting needle from the front to back between the first and second stitches of the first row. Wind the yarn around the needle and pull through a loop to form the new stitch. Normally you have more gaps between rows than stitches you need to pick up and knit. To make sure your picking up is even, you will have to miss a gap every few rows.

ALONG A CAST-ON OR BOUND- (CAST-) OFF EDGE
This is worked in the same way as picking up stitches along a vertical edge, except that you will work through the cast-on stitches rather than the gaps between rows. You will normally have the same number of stitches to pick up and knit as there are existing stitches.

slipping stitches

This means moving stitches from one needle to the other without knitting or purling them. They can be slipped knitwise or purlwise depending on the row you are working, or any specific pattern instructions.

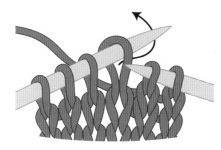

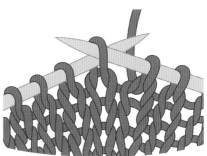

KNITWISE
From left to right, put the right-hand needle into the next stitch on the left-hand needle (as shown by the arrow) and slip it across onto the right-hand needle without working it.

PURLWISE
You can slip a stitch purlwise on a purl row or a knit row. From right to left, put the right-hand needle into the next stitch on the left-hand needle and slip it across onto the right-hand needle without working it.

yarnover (yo)

To make a yarnover, wind the yarn around the right-hand needle to make an extra loop that is worked as a stitch on the next row.

Bring the yarn between the tips of the needles to the front. Take the yarn over the right-hand needle to the back and knit the next stitch on the left-hand needle (see page 117).

Be sure not to confuse "yo" with the abbreviations "yf" or "yb," both of which are used in this book (see page 127 for explanations of these terms).

increasing

There are four methods of increasing used in projects in this book.

INCREASE ON A KNIT ROW (INC)

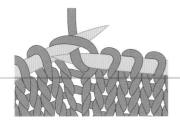

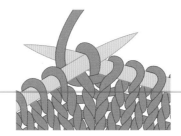

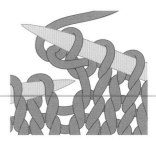

1 Knit the next stitch on the left-hand needle in the usual way (see page 117), but do not slip the "old" stitch off the left-hand needle.

2 Move the right-hand needle behind the left-hand needle and put it into the same stitch again, but through the back of the stitch this time. Knit the stitch again.

3 Now slip the "old" stitch off the left-hand needle in the usual way.

INCREASE ON A PURL ROW (INC PWISE)

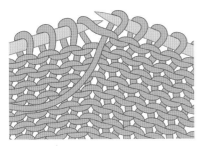

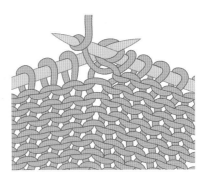

1 Purl the next stitch on the left-hand needle in the usual way (see page 118), but do not slip the "old" stitch off the left-hand needle.

2 Twist the right-hand needle backward to make it easier to put it into the same stitch again, but through the back of the stitch this time. Purl the stitch again, then slip the "old" stitch off the left-hand needle in the usual way.

MAKE ONE STITCH (M1)

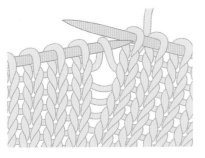

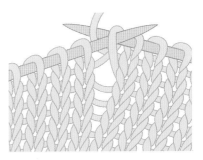

1 From the front, slip the tip of the left-hand needle under the horizontal strand of yarn running between the last stitch on the right-hand needle and the first stitch on the left-hand needle.

2 Put the right-hand needle knitwise into the back of the loop formed by the picked-up strand and knit into it in the normal way. (It is important to knit into the back of the loop so that it is twisted and a hole does not form in your work.)

MAKE ONE STITCH BELOW (M1 BELOW)

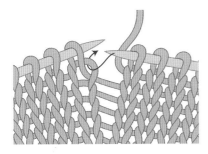

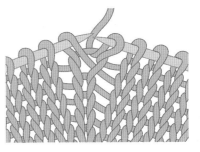

1 Find the top loop of the stitch below the next stitch on the left-hand needle. Insert the tip of the right-hand needle into that top loop from front to back. If this is difficult try picking up the stitch from the back, hold it with the left thumb and forefinger, then remove the needle and reinsert it into the loop from front to back.

2 Knit into the stitch, then knit into the next stitch on the left-hand needle in the usual way.

decreasing

There are four different ways of decreasing used in this book.

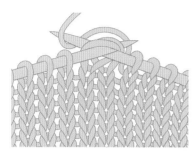 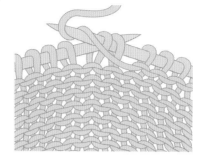 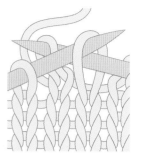

KNIT TWO TOGETHER (K2TOG)
This is the simplest way of decreasing. Simply insert the right-hand needle through two stitches instead of the normal one, and then knit them in the usual way.

The same principle is used to knit three stitches together; just insert the right-hand needle through three stitches instead of through two.

PURL TWO TOGETHER (P2TOG)
To make a simple decrease on a purl row, insert the right-hand needle through two stitches instead of the normal one, and then purl them in the usual way (see page 118).
This decrease can also be worked through the back of the stitch loops to make "p2tog tbl."

SLIP ONE, KNIT ONE, PASS THE SLIPPED STITCH OVER (SKPO)
Slip the first stitch knitwise from the left-hand to the right-hand needle without knitting it (see page 120). Knit the next stitch. Then lift the slipped stitch over the knitted stitch and drop it off the needle.

SLIP, SLIP, KNIT (SSK)
1 Slip one stitch knitwise, and then the next stitch knitwise onto the right-hand needle, without knitting them.

2 Insert the left-hand needle from left to right through the front loops of both the slipped stitches and knit them in the usual way.

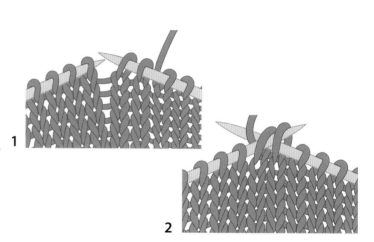

knitting in different colors

It's important to change colors in the right way to keep the knitted fabric flat and smooth and without any holes or gaps.

STRANDING
If you are knitting just a few stitches in a different color, you can simply leave the color you are not using on the wrong side of the work and pick it up again when you need to.

CHANGING COLOR ON A KNIT ROW
1 Knit the stitches (see page 117) in color A (brown in this example), bringing the yarn across over the strand of color B (lime in this example) to wrap around the needle.

2 At the color change, drop color A and pick up color B, bringing it across under the strand of color A to wrap around the needle. Be careful not to pull it too tight. Knit the stitches in color B. When you change back to color A, bring it across over the strand of color B.

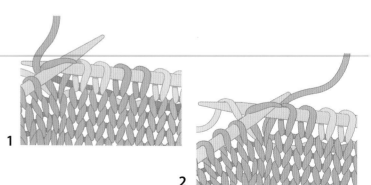

CHANGING COLOR ON A PURL ROW

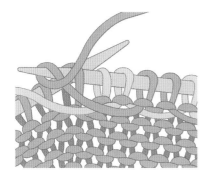

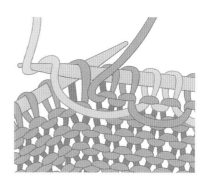

1 Purl the stitches (see page 118) in color A (brown in this example), bringing it across over the strand of color B (lime in this example) to wrap around the needle.

2 At the color change, drop color A and pick up color B, bringing it across under the strand of color A to wrap around the needle. Be careful not to pull it too tight. Purl the stitches in color B. When you change back to color A, bring it across over the strand of color B.

INTARSIA

If you are knitting blocks of different colors within a project then you will need to use a technique called intarsia. This involves having separate balls of yarn for each area and twisting the yarns together where they join to avoid creating a hole or gap.

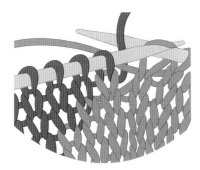

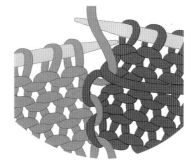

ON THE RIGHT SIDE

When you want to change colors and the color change is vertical or sloping to the right, take the first color over the second color. Then pick up the second color, so the strands of yarn cross each other.

ON THE WRONG SIDE

On this side it is easy to see how the yarns must be interlinked at each color change. This is worked in almost the same way as on the right side. When you want to change colors and the color change is vertical or sloping to the left, take the first color over the second color. Then pick up the second color, so the strands of yarn cross each other.

embroidery stitches

The dolls' features are embroidered using knitting yarn. When embroidering on knitting, take the embroidery needle in and out of the work between the strands that make up the yarn rather than between the knitted stitches themselves; this will help make your embroidery look more even.

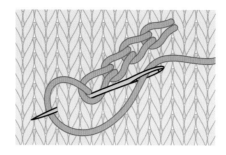

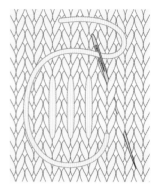

CHAIN STITCH

Bring the yarn out at the starting point on the front of the work. Take the needle back into the knitting just next to the starting point, leaving a loop of yarn. Bring the needle out of the work again, a stitch length further on and catch the loop under it. Pull the thread up firmly, but not so tight that it pulls the knitting. Continue in this way until the stitching is complete.

STRAIGHT STITCH

To make this stitch, simply take the yarn out at the starting point and back down into the work where you want the stitch to end.
To work satin stitch, work straight stitches very close together.

FRENCH KNOT

1 Bring the yarn out at the starting point, where you want the French knot to sit. Wind the yarn around the needle twice, or three times for a larger knot.

2 Take the needle back into the work, just to the side of the starting point. Gently pull the needle and yarn through the work and slide the knot off the needle and onto the knitting, pulling it taut. Then bring the needle out at the point for the next French knot or, if you are working a single knot, secure it on the back.

LAZY DAISY

1 Bringing the yarn out where the center of the flower will be, make a single chain stitch (see above), and anchor the loop in place with a tiny straight stitch.

2 Repeat Step 1 to make a daisy flower with as many petals as required.

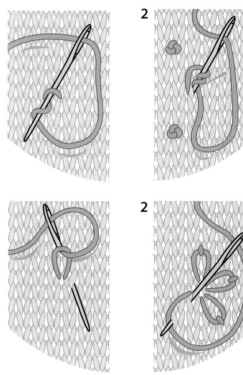

EMBROIDERING

For marking the position of eyes before you embroider them, glass-headed pins can be useful. A water-soluble pen is useful to mark the position of the nose and mouth.

When embroidering features, use a pointed embroidery needle, not the round-ended one used for sewing your work together.

Start off your embroidery by tying a knot in the end of the yarn and taking the yarn between stitches in an

inconspicuous place, such as the back of the head. Pull gently so the knot disappears into the doll. Finish off in a similar way, working a couple of tiny stitches, one over the other, round the running thread between knitted stitches.

Conceal the yarn tails on stuffed items within the item itself by taking the yarn into the item and out again. Squash the item slightly, pull the yarn taut, and trim it close to your knitting. When the item regains shape, the yarn tail will disappear into the doll or animal.

SWISS EMBROIDERY

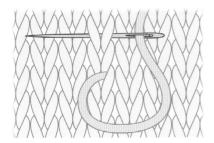 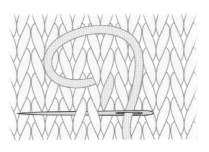 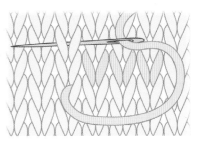

1 To work a horizontal line, start at the right-hand end. Bring the yarn out at the base of a stitch to be embroidered, then slip the needle around the top of the stitch, going under the "legs" of the stitch above.

2 Take the needle back through the base of the stitch and gently tighten the yarn so it covers the knitted stitch. Bring the needle out at the base of the next stitch to the left.

3 Continue to work along the row of knitted stitches in this way, covering each one with an embroidered stitch.

crochet chain

A few projects require a simple crochet chain.

1 Make a slip knot on the crochet hook in the same way as for knitting (see page 116). Holding the slip stitch on the hook, wind the yarn around the hook from the back to the front, then catch the yarn in the crochet-hook tip.

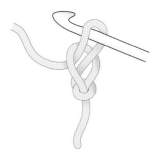

2 Pull the yarn through the slip stitch on the crochet hook to make the second link in the chain. Continue in this way till the chain is the length needed.

sewing seams

There are various sewing-up stitches, and the patterns advise you on which method to use.

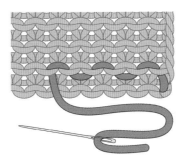 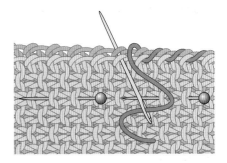

SEWING IN ENDS
The easiest way to finish yarn ends is to run a few small stitches forward then backward through your work, ideally in a seam. Use a pointed needle because working between the individual strands that make up the yarn can help the yarn tail stay put.

OVERSEWING
This stitch can be worked with the right or the wrong sides of the work together. Thread a yarn sewing needle with a tail left after binding (casting) off, or a long length of yarn. Bring the yarn from the back of the work, over the edge of the knitting, and out through to the back again a short distance further on.

MATTRESS STITCH ON ROW-END EDGES

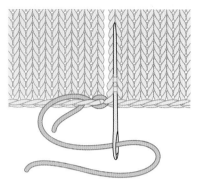

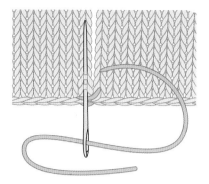

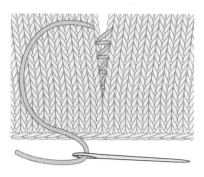

1 Right-sides up, lay the edges to be joined side by side. Thread a yarn sewing needle and from the back, bring it up between the first and second stitches of the left-hand piece, immediately above the cast-on edge. Take it across to the right-hand piece, and from the back bring it through between the first two stitches, immediately above the cast-on edge. Take it back to the left-hand piece and from the back, bring it through where it first came out. Pull the yarn through and this figure-eight will hold the cast-on edges level. Take the needle across to the right-hand piece and, from the front, take it under the bars of yarn between the first and second stitches on the next two rows up.

2 Take the needle across to the left-hand piece and, from the front, take it under the bars of yarn between the first and second stitches on the next two rows up. Continue in this way, taking the needle under two bars on one piece and then the other, to sew up the seam.

3 When you have sewn about 1in (2.5cm), gently and evenly pull the stitches tight to close the seam, and then continue to complete the sewing.

SEWING UP
When sewing your knitted pieces together, use a round-ended needle to avoid splitting the yarn. And don't rush or cut corners. For example, pinning on a doll's hair before stitching it in place really will save time and hassle in the long run.

MATTRESS STITCH ON CAST-ON AND BOUND- (CAST-) OFF EDGES

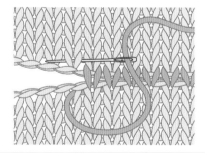

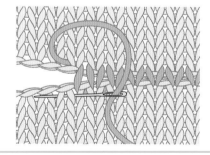

1 Right-sides up, lay the two edges to be joined side by side. Thread a yarn sewing needle with a tail left after binding (casting) off, or a long length of yarn.
Secure the yarn on the back of the lower knitted piece, then bring the needle up through the middle of the first whole stitch in that piece. Take the needle under both "legs" of the first whole stitch on the upper piece, so that it comes to the front between the first and second stitches.

2 Go back into the lower piece and take the needle through to the back where it first came out, and then bring it back to the front in the middle of the next stitch along. Pull the yarn through. Take the needle under both "legs" of the next whole stitch on the upper piece. Repeat this step to sew the seam. Pull the stitches gently taut to close the seam as you work.

abbreviations

approx.	approximately
beg	begin(ning)
cm	centimeter(s)
cont	continue
g	gram(s)
in	inch(es)
inc	increase on a knit row, by working into front and back of next stitch: see page 120
inc pwise	increase on a purl row, by working into front and back of next stitch: see page 121
k	knit
k2tog	knit two stitches together: see page 122
k3tog	knit three stitches together: see page 122
kwise	knitwise
m1	make one stitch, by knitting into the strand between two stitches: see page 121
m	meter(s)
mm	millimeter
oz	ounces
p	purl
patt	pattern
p2tog	purl two stitches together, see page 122
psso	pass slipped stitch over, pass a slipped stitch over another stitch
p2sso	pass two slipped stitches over, pass two slipped stitches over another stitch
pwise	purlwise
rem	remain(ing)
rep	repeat
RS	right side
skpo	slip one stitch, knit one stitch, pass slipped stitch over knitted one, to decrease: see page 122
sl1(2)	slip one (two) stitch(es), from left- to right-hand needle without knitting it (them): see page 120. If two, slip them together.
ssk	slip one stitch, slip one stitch, knit slipped stitches together, to decrease: see page 122
st(s)	stitch(es)
st st	stockinette (stocking) stitch
tbl	through back loop: work through the back of the stitch
WS	wrong side
yb	yarn back, between the tips of the needles
yd	yard(s)
yf	yarn forward, between the tips of the needles
yo	yarnover, wrap yarn around needle between stitches, to increase and to make an eyelet: see page 120
[ ]	work instructions within square brackets as directed
*	work instructions after/between asterisk(s) as directed

suppliers

The yarn used throughout this book is Debbie Bliss Baby Cashmerino, which is available online from Love Knitting:

Love Knitting
www.loveknitting.com
Online sales

For alternative yarn suggestions, see the box on page 115. On the right is a list of some other major yarn suppliers for alternative yarns and knitting equipment, but for reasons of space we cannot cover all stockists, so please explore the local knitting shops and online stores in your own country.

USA

Knitting Fever Inc.
www.knittingfever.com
Stockist locator on website

WEBS
www.yarn.com

UK

John Lewis
Retail stores and online
Tel: 03456 049049
www.johnlewis.com
Telephone numbers of stores on website

Laughing Hens
Online store only
Tel: +44 (0) 1829 740903
www.laughinghens.com

AUSTRALIA

Black Sheep Wool 'n' Wares
Retail store and online
Tel: +61 (0)2 6779 1196
www.blacksheepwool.com.au

Sun Spun
Retail store only (Canterbury, Victoria)
Tel: +61 (0)3 9830 1609

index

author acknowledgments

I would like to thank Cindy Richards, Penny Craig, Sally Powell, Kerry Lewis, and everyone at CICO Books for taking the idea for this book on board and being so professional. I'd also like to thank my editor Kate Haxell, pattern checker Marilyn Wilson, book designer Luana Gobbo, photographer Geoff Dann, and stylist Nel Haynes for their hard work and brilliant ideas. Last but not least, thanks to my husband, Roger Dromard, for putting up with a house that looks like a wool shop and the near-constant sound of clicking needles.